Interactive IR User Study Design, Evaluation, and Reporting

Synthesis Lectures on Information Concepts, Retrieval, and Services

Editor
Gary Marchionini, *University of North Carolina at Chapel Hill*

Synthesis Lectures on Information Concepts, Retrieval, and Services publishes short books on topics pertaining to information science and applications of technology to information discovery, production, distribution, and management. Potential topics include: data models, indexing theory and algorithms, classification, information architecture, information economics, privacy and identity, scholarly communication, bibliometrics and webometrics, personal information management, human information behavior, digital libraries, archives and preservation, cultural informatics, information retrieval evaluation, data fusion, relevance feedback, recommendation systems, question answering, natural language processing for retrieval, text summarization, multimedia retrieval, multilingual retrieval, and exploratory search.

Interactive IR User Study Design, Evaluation, and Reporting
Jiqun Liu and Chirag Shah

Predicting Information Retrieval Performance
Robert M. Losee

Framing Privacy in Digital Collections with Ethical Decision Making
Virginia Dressler

Mobile Search Behaviors: An In-depth Analysis Based on Contexts, APPs, and Devices
Dan Wu and Shaobo Liang

Images in Social Media: Categorization and Organization of Images and Their Collections
Susanne Ørnager and Haakon Lund

Exploring Context in Information Behavior: Seeker, Situation, Surroundings, and Shared Identities
Naresh Kumar Agarwal

Researching Serendipity in Digital Information Environments
Lori McCay-Peet and Elaine G. Toms

Social Monitoring for Public Health
Michael J. Paul and Mark Dredze

Automated Metadata in Multimedia Information Systems: Creation, Refinement, Use in Surrogates, and Evaluation

Michael G. Christel

Interactive IR User Study Design, Evaluation, and Reporting
Jiqun Liu and Chirag Shah

ISBN: 978-3-031-01191-7 Paperback
ISBN: 978-3-031-02319-4 eBook
ISBN: 978-3-031-00226-7 Hardcover

DOI 10.1007/978-3-031-02319-4

A Publication in the Springer series
SYNTHESIS LECTURES ON INFORMATION CONCEPTS, RETRIEVAL, AND SERVICES
Lecture #67

Series Editor: Gary Marchionini, University of North Carolina, Chapel Hill

Series ISSN 1947-945X   Print   1947-9468 Electronic

Interactive IR User Study Design, Evaluation, and Reporting

Jiqun Liu and Chirag Shah
Rutgers University

SYNTHESIS LECTURES ON INFORMATION CONCEPTS, RETRIEVAL, AND SERVICES #67

ABSTRACT

Since user study design has been widely applied in search interactions and information retrieval (IR) systems evaluation studies, a deep reflection and meta-evaluation of interactive IR (IIR) user studies is critical for sharpening the instruments of IIR research and improving the reliability and validity of the conclusions drawn from IIR user studies. To this end, we developed a faceted framework for supporting user study design, reporting, and evaluation based on a systematic review of the state-of-the-art IIR research papers recently published in several top IR venues (n=462). Within the framework, we identify three major types of research focuses, extract and summarize facet values from specific cases, and highlight the under-reported user study components which may significantly affect the results of research. Then, we employ the faceted framework in evaluating a series of IIR user studies against their respective research questions and explain the roles and impacts of the underlying connections and "collaborations" among different facet values. Through bridging diverse combinations of facet values with the study design decisions made for addressing research problems, the faceted framework can shed light on IIR user study design, reporting, and evaluation practices and help students and young researchers design and assess their own studies.

KEYWORDS

interactive information retrieval, user studies, faceted approach, evaluation, controlled laboratory study, field study, human-information interaction, information seeking and retrieval, user study reporting practice

Contents

Preface

According to the cognitive viewpoint of information retrieval (IR) research, IR systems are essentially interactive and thus users should not be abstracted out of system evaluations. To understand the role of users in IR and to evaluate systems with users, interactive IR (IIR) researchers usually design user studies in different contexts (i.e., controlled laboratory and naturalistic settings) to examine various elements, facets, and stages of information search and evaluation process. Since user study approach has been widely applied in search behavior and IR systems evaluation studies, an effective evaluation framework of IIR user studies is critical for sharpening the instruments of IIR research and improving the reliability and validity of the conclusions drawn from IIR user studies. Despite the longstanding emphasis on evaluation in the IR community, there is still a lack of evaluation of user studies as such, which hinders the fusion of the rigor of classical IR experimentation and the richness of users' search interactions. This book is an attempt to highlight this research gap, synthesize literature around it, and engage the readers in thinking through some of the ways forward.

We start by presenting a faceted framework for user study evaluation based on a systematic review of the state-of-the-art IIR research papers published in ACM SIGIR conferences (2000–2018), CHIIR conferences (2016–2018), *Journal of the Association for Information Science and Technology* (*JASIST*), *Information Processing and Management* (*IP&M*), CHI conferences, and *ACM Transactions on Information Systems (ACM TOIS)* in Chapters 2 and 3. Note that we only included the user studies where researchers proposed IIR-related research questions, recruited participants, and clearly articulated the major components of study design (e.g., experimental system, task, test collection), aiming to ensure that the detailed information concerning user study design can be properly collected and analyzed.

Within the proposed faceted evaluation framework, in Chapter 4 we identify three major types of research focuses based on the literature review in Chapter 2 (i.e., understanding user behavior and experience, system/interface features evaluation, and meta-evaluation of evaluation metrics) and explain how different facets and factors are employed and combined to jointly support the explorations on different research problems. Also, we highlight the under-reported user study facets (e.g., language, participant incentives, pilot study), which may significantly affect the results and the associated findings of research. Then, in Chapter 5 we employ the proposed faceted framework and examine the strengths and weaknesses of a series of IIR user studies by (1) evaluating the value and quality of each individual facet values (e.g., task type, system components), and (2) evaluating the connections and "collaborations" among different facets (e.g., the relationship between participant and task context; the connection between study design and statistical methods). In addition, we emphasize that for evaluation-oriented user studies, it is also critical for researchers to evaluate the ground truth measures in order to make sure the evaluation of system features or evaluation metrics are built upon solid empirical basis.

Although the faceted evaluation of IIR user studies can help improve the instruments of user-oriented IIR studies and thereby broaden the territory of IIR research, it does not mean that there is a single best toolkit for user studies which can be universally applied for all IIR-related research questions. As Stephen Robertson notes in his *Journal of Information Science* paper titled "On the History of Evaluation in IR" (2008, p.447), "In the end, any experimental design is a compromise, a matter of balancing those aspects which are felt to be necessary for a good result." The ultimate goal of this work is to evaluate different types of design decisions and compromises in user studies with respect to their contributions to answering the proposed corresponding research questions.

When deconstructing a user study as a complex entity via a faceted approach, we can conceptualize every specific user study as a particular combination of interrelated facet values. Through bridging diverse combinations of facet values with the study design decisions and compromises made for addressing research problems, this book makes the following contributions.

- It offers a comprehensive picture of various facets of the state-of-the-art IIR user study design in a variety of research contexts.

- The faceted evaluation framework sheds light on both user study evaluation and future standard IIR study practice and resource (e.g., data, technique) preservation.

- This work highlights the roles of and the relationships among different facets and factors of user studies, and thus may help improve user study reporting practices in IIR community.

Chapters 6 and 7 discuss in detail the implications and challenges associated with the proposed faceted framework on multiple aspects of user study practices. By carefully examining the facets of user studies and the underlying connections among them, this work can encourage students, researchers, and practitioners in the IIR community to reflect on the roles and potential of user studies in understanding the interactions between people, information, and search systems. Also, it can enhance our understanding of the structure and the related impacts of the "decisions in compromise" and better support the dialectic around IIR user study design, reporting, and evaluation practices.

Acknowledgments

We are grateful to Dr. Gary Marchionini for his support on this book. We also greatly appreciate the insightful comments and suggestions provided by Drs. Nicholas J. Belkin, Max L. Wilson, Heather O'Brien, and Jacek Gwizdka. Finally, we are thankful for the help and support of Diane Cerra from Morgan & Claypool Publishers. Our studies that inspired and empirically supported this work were funded by NSF grants IIS-1423239 and IIS-1717488.

Jiqun Liu and Chirag Shah, May 2019

CHAPTER 1

Introduction

We are living in an *information age* where various information systems, devices, and recommendations are becoming ubiquitous. The ubiquity of systems and available information supports the diverse interactions of people with information within a variety of environments and largely expands the role of Information Retrieval (IR) in modern society. Specifically, the adoption and usage of search systems have gone beyond traditional libraries and workplaces and have become increasingly more common in everyday-life situations (e.g., checking weather before travel, finding a nearby gas station, checking the distance between a conference venue and the airport). New modes and interfaces of information retrieval (e.g., mobile search, spoken/conversational search, tangible information retrieval) continue to emerge from the development of a series of cutting-edge technologies (e.g., Jansen et al., 2010; Kamvar and Baluja, 2006; Trippas et al., 2018; White, 2018).

Given the importance of IR systems in connecting people with information, it is critical for both researchers and system designers to understand: (1) how users interact with systems in information search and retrieval; (2) the contextual factors (e.g., task, information seeking intention, personality traits) that motivate them to engage in the interaction with information and system. In addition, since IR systems are often built as "bridges" for connecting users with useful information in the right contexts, we also need to explore how we should evaluate these "bridges," especially in different task contexts and problematic situations.

Decades of IR research has been conducted to address different aspects of these questions in many research communities, such as information seeking, human-computer interaction, and information retrieval research communities. Among different approaches to answering these central questions concerning human information interaction, IIR (IIR) research differs from classical system-oriented IR research in that it adopts a cognitive viewpoint and focuses on the user's role in information interaction and IR system evaluation (Belkin, 1990). IIR user study as a combination of a series of interrelated components and techniques has been serving as a useful toolkit for researchers in investigations of user behavior (e.g., querying, browsing, evaluation) at multiple levels (i.e., behavioral level, cognitive level, affective level) and explorations of the context of human information interaction (Kelly, 2009). Despite the strength in revealing contextual features and user characteristics, IIR user study also presents a new challenge to study design evaluation and reporting practices as many of the study components are unique and only applicable in certain research contexts.

The challenge in user study evaluation can be deconstructed into following questions. What are the major dimensions and facets of IIR user study toolkit? What are the relationships among them in IR studies? How can we properly evaluate user studies of different types based on the corresponding research problems they are designed to address? Answering these questions and building a framework for characterizing and evaluating IIR user studies can help us better reflect on the roles and effects of different components, methods, and techniques in user-oriented IR studies and thus can further improve our understanding of human information interaction in IR context.

1.1   BACKGROUND: USER STUDY IN IIR RESEARCH

The term *user study* in the area of information science originally refers to the studies that explore human information seeking needs (Kelly, 2009). In contemporary research studies, due to the growth of information behavior community and the diversification of user-oriented research problems and techniques, user study is defined more generally to describe any study that involves human participants. Within this broad scope of research, different types of user studies can be placed at different positions in a research continuum that is anchored by human focused studies and system focused studies (cf. Kelly, 2009), depending on the nature of their main research focuses. This wide range of user study type demonstrates that user study as a research methodology has the potential to help address a variety of research questions which are directly or indirectly related to user-oriented search system design and evaluation. Note that some of the user studies published in IR community are not directly associated with any of the system components in IIR evaluation (e.g., Moshfeghi, Triantafillou, and Pollick, 2016). Instead, they focused on some more fundamental concepts (e.g., information need, relevance, anomalous state of knowledge) that form the theoretical and empirical basis of user modeling and user-centered system design and evaluation.

According to the cognitive viewpoint of IR research, information search and retrieval is essentially interactive, thus users should not be abstracted out of IR system evaluation (Belkin, 1990; Ingwersen, 1996). Built upon this premise, IIR user study brings user factors into system evaluation and puts IR problems into the broader research context of human information interaction. Because of the complexity of user behavior, many different facets of user study are considered and examined in study design, reporting, and result interpretation. Also, a series of new techniques and methods (e.g., eye tracker, functional magnetic resonance imaging) are employed to capture user features (e.g., Moshfeghi, Triantafillou, and Pollick, 2016; Cole et al., 2013). Given the role and potential of user studies in understanding users' interactions with IR systems, examining and synthesizing the facets of user studies can enhance our understanding of IIR research methodology, help us address the aforementioned questions associated with user study evaluation.

1.2   AIM OF THE WORK

As Robertson notes, "In the end, any experimental design is a compromise, a matter of balancing those aspects which the experimenter feels should be realistic with those controls which are felt to be necessary for a good result" (Robertson, 2008, p. 447). This balance among different facets is much more difficult to reach in user studies than in classical system-focused IR evaluations, primarily because of various individual differences and the dynamic nature of human cognition, perception, and associated behaviors during the course of information seeking episodes. Therefore, the aims of this work on IIR user studies evaluation are:

- identify the facets/dimensions of user study, especially the easily ignored user-side factors which may significantly alter the results of study; and

- evaluate the strengths and limitations of different types of designs and compromises made in user studies with respect to answering their respective research questions.

Indeed, there is no single best toolkit for user studies which can be universally applied for all IIR-related research problems. However, it is still beneficial for researchers to be clear about: (1) given the research problem(s), what kind of balance they hope and need to reach among different dimensions or facets of user study; and (2) what are the potential impacts of the decisions and compromises made in user study design on the associated results and findings?

1.3   SYSTEMATIC REVIEW AND USER STUDY EVALUATION

In this work, our approach to developing knowledge and addressing the research problems discussed above is to build a faceted framework and apply it in deconstructing, characterizing, and evaluating various types of IIR user studies. To develop and implement the faceted approach, we first systematically reviewed and collected 462 IIR user study papers published in multiple high-quality IR venues. Then, we developed an initial faceted framework from a small portion of the selected papers and revised and updated when new factors and facets emerged or being extracted from the paper coding process.

In terms of the criteria of paper selection, we only included the user studies where researchers proposed IIR-related research questions, recruited participants (instead of using simulated users), and clearly articulated the major components of their study design (e.g., experimental system, task design, test collection and corpus, interface). Hence, user studies where researchers only used search behavior datasets from the existing user study collections (e.g., Text Retrieval Conference (TREC) test collections,[1] NII Testbeds and Community for Information access Research (NTCIR) test collections [2]), or large-scale search logs (e.g., Bing search logs, Yandex search logs) without designing any new study were excluded from our analysis as they did not really pertain to the dilemma of balancing different facets and making difficult compromises in user study design (e.g., Deveaud et al., 2018; Feild and Allan, 2013; Jiang et al., 2017; Luo, Zhang, and Yang, 2014; Spink et al., 2004).

---

[1] https://trec.nist.gov/
[2] http://research.nii.ac.jp/ntcir/index-en.html

One may argue that this type of *user study* did deal with the issue of study design compromise in the sense that the researchers faced the trade-off between the richness of user features and data sufficiency in large-scale search logs. However, this is not the type of compromise we are interested in here. More details regarding paper selection and the development of faceted framework are reported in Chapters 3 and 4.

When the paper coding process was completed, we applied the faceted framework in characterizing and evaluating IIR user studies of different types. The user study evaluation roughly follows three steps.

1. Given a specific user study case, we first identify the research focus (e.g., understanding user behavior, evaluating new interface component) as well as the specific research problems.

2. Based on the step 1, we identify the main facets and the associated sub-facets and factors from the faceted evaluation framework. Specifically, we mainly focus on the factors that are manipulated in the study (e.g., size of the search engine result page, search assistance) and the facets that are associated with the variables of interest (e.g., task features, user characteristics, mode of search, stage of search session). Also, we look at the facets that need to be controlled given the research context.

3. More importantly, we explore the connections among different facets and evaluate the compromises made in user study design based on the research questions proposed in the paper. The decisions and compromises in study design are usually made for the purpose of obtaining benefits from other aspects and facets. Our hope is that the faceted approach proposed here can at least help researchers qualitatively understand and evaluate the role of different facets and the compromises made by researchers in balancing different facets or dimensions and ultimately in answering the proposed research questions. More details regarding the faceted scheme of IIR user studies are provided with specific examples in Chapters 5 and 6.

1.4   IMPLICATIONS OF THE FACETED FRAMEWORK

When deconstructing a user study as a complex entity via a faceted or multidimensional approach, we can define every specific user study as a unique vector of different facet values corresponding to different user study components. Through building a faceted framework for depicting and evaluation IIR user study, this book makes the following contributions.

• It offers a comprehensive picture of various facets of the state-of-the-art user study design in a variety of research contexts.

- The faceted framework sheds light on user study reporting, evaluation and future standard IIR study practice and resource (e.g., data, system components and techniques, study procedure) preservation.

- Most importantly, this work highlights the roles of and the relationships among different facets of user studies, and thus may help improve user study reporting practices in the IR community.

It is worth noting that the comprehensiveness of our framework refers to the broad coverage and representativeness of the facets extracted from existing IIR user studies, rather than the exhaustiveness with our coverage of the past literature. In other words, we are not trying to review and annotate all available user study papers published in IIR-related venues so far. Despite the difference in specific research problems and subjects, a large body of IR research actually adopted a very similar set of study protocols and methodologies. In this work we seek to develop a faceted framework that can cover and capture most, if not all, of the facets and factors of user study as well as the connections among these facets.

As Robertson (2008) points out, "a field advances not by deciding on a single best compromise, but through different researchers taking different decisions, and the resulting dialectic" (p. 447). In the recent two decades, the diversity in user study design decisions (e.g., participant recruitment, task design, study device, data collection) largely supports the explorations of users' interactions with IR systems in context and significantly expands the entire scope of IIR research. By carefully examining the facets of user studies and the relations among them, this work can enhance our understanding of the structure and the related impacts of the "decision in compromise" and better support the dialectic around IIR user study design, reporting, and evaluation practices.

CHAPTER 2

Interactive Information Retrieval

In today's information-intensive living environments, extracting useful information from large-scale electronic resources is not only one of the main online activities of individuals, but also a key skill for professional groups to accomplish goals in workplaces of different types (Ruthven, 2008). IIR research looks at the interaction between people and search systems in various task scenarios, and seeks to (1) understand how users interact with systems and why do they interact in such ways (e.g., Cole et al., 2014; He and Yilmaz, 2017; Liu et al., 2019; Ong et al., 2017); and (2) how should we evaluate IR systems of different types with users (e.g., Azzopardi, Kelly, and Brennan, 2013; Kato et al., 2014; Kelly, 2009). Moreover, researchers seek to leverage the knowledge about user and task characteristics they learned from user studies in the design and implementation of system recommendations and interventions for people's work and search tasks which contextualize their information seeking and search practices (e.g., Ahn et al., 2008; Liu, Belkin, and Cole., 2012; Shah, 2018).

Since the pioneers who participated in the TREC interactive track developed IIR evaluation methods from the user's perspective, IIR research has flourished over the past decade due to the emergence of numerous innovative systems, tools, and user-oriented evaluation measures. Despite the rapid growth of IIR user study practices in a wide range of problem spaces, there have been very few studies taking a step back and reflecting on the evolving facets of user studies themselves. This lack of meta-evaluation of study design (especially the connections between different facets and components), to some extent, hinders the development of standard user study practices, and thereby damages the reliability and replicability of IIR research. This replicability crisis becomes even worse when researchers go beyond the standard TREC-like practice and adopt innovative components, unique techniques, and procedures in user study design for some specific research problems and contexts (e.g., type of workspace, user population, task type). Therefore, given the diversity of existing research problems, methods, and techniques, a relatively standard characterization and evaluation of user studies as diverse combinations of a series of different facet values is desperately needed in the IIR community as well as in the information behavior community in general.

2.1   BACKGROUND

Kelly (2009) offers a comprehensive overview of the research approaches, methods, and techniques regarding the evaluation of IR systems with users, which helps form the basis (i.e., initial fundamental facets) for our faceted evaluation framework. In this overview, several major components of

IIR user studies (e.g., research approaches, sampling, task and experimental design, measures and data analysis) are discussed in detail in separate sections. Furthermore, given the lack of meta-evaluation on methods and measures, Kelly (2009) calls for more serious scholarship and research efforts devoted specifically to the reflection and meta-analysis on IIR user studies. While Kelly provides a comprehensive review of the methods and techniques employed in user studies published before 2009, updates are needed especially with respect to the newly developed techniques, methods and study procedures and how they have been applied to both classical IR problems (e.g., Moshfeghi, Triantafillou, and Pollick, 2016) and novel research issues (e.g., Büschel, Mitschick, and Dachselt, 2018; Edwards and Kelly, 2017; Lagun et al, 2014). Besides, since Kelly (2009) describes a generic structure and discusses different factors and aspects in separate sections, the study design decisions on how to combine different facet values as a whole in specific research contexts are still not clear. Therefore, to better support the dialectic around the study design decisions of different types, include new dimensions and techniques, and properly characterize and evaluate IIR user studies, we need to develop a more comprehensive framework and to clarify the underlying relations among different facets in different research scenarios as well as the rationales behind various study design decisions and compromises between interrelated facets (e.g., remove the restriction on the task time length in order to obtain more natural reactions from users in terms of search behavior).

Kelly and Sugimoto (2013) provides a systematic review of 40 years (1967–2006) of IIR evaluation studies and identifies a series of research method features which are highly relevant to our present study. Based on the analysis of 127 journal and conference papers selected from 2,791 papers within the time period, Kelly and Sugimoto (2013) documents the evolution of IIR evaluation methods and experimental design and argue that task-based and user-centered evaluations pose difficult problems for both existing and future user studies. Their work also indicates that divergent and sometimes poor reporting practices make it extremely difficult, if not completely impossible, to conduct effective meta-evaluation on existing IIR studies and findings. Similar to Kelly (2009), Kelly and Sugimoto (2013) summarize the research method features separately and does not explicitly discuss the underlying associations among different features and aspects. Furthermore, because of the limitations in the reporting practices of the reviewed IIR papers, Kelly and Sugimoto (2013) report on only a narrow range of generic method features, including number of subjects, tasks, corpora, and measures employed in search system evaluation. To understand and evaluate a user study, it is necessary to identify the major facets that may affect the findings and results, and also to figure out how these facets and dimensions "collaborate" with each other in helping answer research question(s).

In addition to the above systematic reviews on IIR studies, there are some review works that focus on one or two aspects of IR study design. For instance, given the strong connection between statistical reporting and the validity of research findings, some previous works have specifically examined the statistical result reporting practices in IR papers, including IIR research (e.g., Sakai, 2016; Sanderson and Zobel, 2005).

According to Sakai (2016), many IR effectiveness papers either lack significance testing or fail to report p-values and/or sample size for power analysis. Similar poor statistical reporting practices are also discussed in Kelly and Sugimoto (2013): "In some cases, the type of test conducted was not reported although statistically significant results were claimed or p-values were presented" (p.766).

To make matters worse, there is the publication bias problem and plenty of the statistically non-significant results were hidden or rejected from peer review and scholarly publication (Sakai, 2016). As a natural extension and presentation of meta-analysis of IIR user studies, study reporting (especially study result reporting) practice is an important aspect that should be carefully examined in an evaluation framework.

To provide clearer guidance and reference for study design and reporting practices, our work seeks to summarize all major facets and associated sub-facets within the same framework, and also to clarify the relations among different facets in different lines of IIR research. When designing user studies to answer IIR research questions, researchers may use our faceted framework to: (1) check if any critical facets or factors are missed out or not controlled, and what are the potential impacts on the result; and (2) reflect on the relations between different facets and see if a reasonable balance is reached between different, and even conflicting facet values. For example, to better control the environment of information search study, researchers may put a series of constraints on users' interactions with the system (e.g., fixed search engine result pages, pre-defined tasks, pre-defined queries, limit on search time length) and thus may not be able to fully elicit natural information seeking behaviors. With respect to user study reporting, researchers can use the faceted framework as a checklist to make sure they at least have all main facets reported and clearly explained so that their results and findings can be interpreted and evaluated in the right manner. Additionally, it would also be easier for other researchers to replicate and reuse the same study procedure in different environments and communities (especially beyond college student communities) and to test the reliability of the research conclusion(s).

At this point it may be worth asking a more fundamental question—what are the current main research lines in the area of IIR? When extracting the research focuses of different types, we classified the IIR research papers into different categories according to their relative position on the research continuum (i.e., whether the main research focus is closer to system sider or human/user side) presented in Kelly (2009) (see Figure 2.1). Based on the analysis of the papers collected from various venues, we identified three major types of research focuses in our framework: *understanding search behavior and experience*, *system/interface features evaluation*, and *meta-evaluation of evaluation metrics*. These three research focuses speak to three different lines of IIR research. It is worth noting that some studies may stand of the intersection between two different problem spaces. In these cases, we classified them based on the primary focus on which they devoted most of their research efforts and resources.

As a preparation for building a faceted scheme of user studies, this chapter discusses in detail the three main lines of research we summarized from previous IIR user studies. Specifically, the following sections discuss the scopes and contributions of IIR studies in the three research lines, respectively. We believe that to properly evaluate a user study it is critical to first understand its central research problem(s) and approaches, and then examine the extent to which the designed user study answers the research question(s) and address the proposed research problem(s).

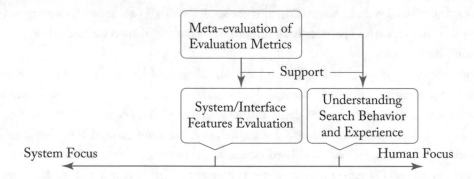

Figure 2.1: IIR research continuum (adapted from Kelly, 2009).

2.2   UNDERSTANDING USER BEHAVIOR AND EXPERIENCE

The user studies that are primarily designed to explicate user behavior and search experiences usually focus on a slice or segment of search process (e.g., query formulation, search result examination, judgment of document relevance) and seek to control other contextual elements of search as much as possible (e.g., document relevance, task complexity). The user studies which fall into this category are generally more interested in explaining or predicting some of the elements associated with user behavior and interaction experience, rather than demonstrating the goodness of a particular system or interface component. In the research continuum shown in Figure 2.1 (see Kelly, 2009), compared to typical IIR evaluation studies, this line of research is clearly closer to the human focus side.

User studies under this category often examine the variations in some of the search contextual features (e.g., task types, stage of search, topical and domain knowledge, number of relevant results on the ranked result lists) and study how users' behavioral signals change when these contextual features vary. For instance, Edwards and Kelly (2017) reports a study on human emotion (i.e., engaged or frustrated) in web search and explains how researchers, to some extent, can manipulate participants' emotional states via controlling task type and the quality of search engine result pages

(SERPs). To examine the explanatory power of Information Foraging Theory, Ong et al. (2017) varied the quality of SERPs to create different information scent levels and patterns and illustrated how this factor of SERP quality affected different aspects of mobile and desktop web search interactions. Aula, Khan, and Guan (2010) asked participants to perform different types of search tasks from a given task pool and demonstrated the effect of task difficulty on query formulation and result examination behaviors. Similarly, Jiang, He, and Allan (2014) examined users' interactions with IR systems in complex search tasks and found that user behaviors vary across different task types in multiple aspects, including search activeness, browsing pattern, result clicking strategy, and query reformulation strategy. In addition, they also demonstrated that as a search session proceeds, users tend to shift their interests to focus less on the top results but more on the results ranked at lower positions on SERPs. Gwizdka (2010) examined users' cognitive loads across different stages of search task using dual-task design and found that users often experience higher cognitive load in query formulation stage compared to other stages. Zhang et al. (2014) also focused on the cognitive aspect of search interaction and demonstrated that a user's domain knowledge level can be inferred from implicit search behavioral measures.

As it is shown in the examples above, to study user characteristics, behavior, and interaction experiences, IIR researchers often manipulate various facets and factors, which often include system features and interface components. However, differing from system-evaluation-focused studies, user studies under this category did not focus on the goodness and usability of the system features varied or newly added interface features. Instead, they intended to change one or two aspects of the search context through manipulating some of the system facets (e.g., SERP quality), and to examine how user react to the changes at different levels and what are the impacts of these changes on users' search experiences (e.g., perceived cognitive load, search satisfaction, user engagement).

The IIR user studies falling into this category have enhanced our understanding of user behavior and experience at different levels (i.e., behavioral level, cognitive level, affective level) and in tasks of different types. In addition to the innovative design and manipulation of core facets (e.g., task, search interface), the adoption of new techniques and measures (e.g., neuro-physiological measures of different types, such as eye movement, brain activity measures, and heart rate measures) also broadens the scope of user behavior and experience research and allows researchers to examine behavioral variations in a more accurate and creative manner. However, to hold "irrelevant" contextual factors under control and to obtain "clear effects" of the facets of interest, researchers need to have a comprehensive, multi-faceted picture of user studies in mind and properly design the constraints and manipulations on different dimensions of user studies. This is where our faceted user study framework should come into play.

2.3 · SYSTEM/INTERFACE FEATURES EVALUATION

The second category (system/interface features evaluation) covers the typical IIR evaluation studies. In this type of work, a human-related, personalized system or interface feature is typically being evaluated. To evaluate systems with users, researchers usually employ multiple methods to collect data on users' search behavior, goal of search, search performance, and the overall experience of search interaction (e.g., in situ questionnaire, post-search questionnaire, individual and focus group interviews) (Kelly, 2009; Moffat et al., 2017). System features designed for user-centered evaluation are often directly related to some of the user characteristics, such as information need, behavior and cognition, and information seeking and search contexts.

Unlike the user studies discussed in the previous section, the system evaluation research usually focus on the added or manipulated system or interface features and evaluate their usefulness and usability in supporting users' interactions with systems in different task contexts. For instance, Syed and Collins-Thompson (2017) designed novel retrieval algorithms to provide personalized results tailored to human learning goals and evaluated the effectiveness of the proposed model on improving word-learning outcomes. In this case, the optimized ranking algorithms were evaluated based on how they shaped the presentation of information and changed participants' knowledge gains in the predefined learning context. Kelly and Fu (2006) focused on term selection in query formulation and examined the usefulness of three relevance feedback interfaces. In the user-centered evaluation, they demonstrated that queries formulated with the help (candidate terms, context of search) from experimental interfaces significantly outperformed corresponding baseline queries. Yuan and Belkin (2007) designed an integrated IIR system which adapts to support different information seeking strategies and indicated that this novel system resulted in significantly better performance in terms of user satisfaction with the retrieved results, effective interaction, and system usability. Dumais et al. (2016) deployed a document finding and re-using system named *Stuff I've Seen* and evaluated the usefulness of the system with employees in Microsoft workplaces. With respect to image search, Xu et al. (2010) developed a novel image search system named *Image Search by Concept Map* and evaluated the effectiveness of the system in supporting users find relevant images.

In the context of computer-supported group work, Hong et al. (2018) explored the possibility of supporting information seeking in the context of group decision-making and demonstrated that providing collaborative dynamic queries to people in groups can significantly improve the group's perceived efficiency, effectiveness, and the level of satisfaction of decision-making process. Similarly, Shah and Marchionini (2010) sought to support explicit collaboration in information seeking activities and found that the system features that support group awareness is critical for effective collaboration and that such support can be applied in information seeking without significantly decreasing system usability or adding additional cognitive loads on the users.

As it is shown above, IIR user studies in this group (system/interface features evaluation) go beyond the classical system-oriented evaluation approach by taking into account users' perception, evaluation, and behavioral pattern in search interaction. The design and evaluation of search systems have been strongly influenced by computer science and algorithmic perspectives for decades. In contrast to traditional IR evaluation works, IIR evaluation take a cognitive, user-centered perspective, put user (instead of explicit query or document) at the central position of search interaction, and evaluate IR system based on the extent to which the system successfully represents user' knowledge states and supports their work and search tasks (Belkin, 2000; Belkin et al., 2004; Ruthven, 2008). To accomplish this goal, researchers need to go beyond explicit queries and ranked documents to capture and represent multiple user-focused facets (e.g., users' knowledge states, task stage, search task difficulty) in search system evaluation.

2.4   META-EVALUATION OF EVALUATION METRICS

In addition to the two major types of IIR user studies discussed above, some of the studies take a step back from specific systems and problems and seek to evaluate the user-oriented measures applied in IR system evaluation. In this type of studies, researchers usually measure user behaviors (e.g., query formulation, search result browsing and examination, eye movement) and experience (e.g., search satisfaction, task difficulty) with different sets of evaluation metrics (e.g., in-situ and post-search evaluation metrics, traditional search behavioral metrics and neuro-physiological metrics) and evaluate the effectiveness of these measures against a series of predefined user-oriented ground truth (e.g., search satisfaction and usefulness judgment). The major goal of this line of studies is to find or design reliable measures that can be applied in future standard IIR evaluation and search interaction studies.

For example, to address the limitations of traditional TREC-style relevance judgments, Jiang, He, and Allan (2017) explored two improvements (i.e., collecting in situ judgment to make relevant judgment contextual; collecting multidimensional assessments to address different aspects of relevance and usefulness) and evaluated the new framework of relevance using six different user experience measures as ground truth. Mao et al. (2016) designed a laboratory study where they compared relevance annotations with document usefulness measures and demonstrated that a measure based on usefulness rather than relevance annotated has a better correlation with user satisfaction. In addition, they also found that external assessors can provide high-quality usefulness annotation when addition search context information was provided to them. Chen et al. (2017) meta-evaluated a series of online and offline metrics (e.g., online behavioral features, offline relevance judgments) to study the extent to which they can infer actual search satisfaction in different task scenarios. As it is shown in the above examples, this line of research sheds light on the connection between user characteristics and IIR evaluation measures and often proposes innovative user-oriented measures that can better integrate IR system evaluation with the measurements of user characteristics, behavior, and interaction experience. Designing useful user-centered evaluation metrics can help support both search behavior studies (e.g., determine which part(s) of search behavior is closely associated with search experience) and search systems evaluation.

2.5   SUMMARY

This chapter introduces the three major streams of research in the area of IIR and illustrates their respective main focuses and topics with recently published IR studies. While the examples of research works presented above cannot exhaust all specific subareas and relevant topics under the three lines of studies, they jointly reveal the diversity of IIR user studies in terms of research problems, methods, topics of interest. Although this growing diversity certainly fosters the vitality of IIR research, it also leads to a series of challenges and obstacles in terms of developing standard IIR practices and unified evaluation framework for user studies. In the following chapters, we will explain how we developed the faceted evaluation framework and how this framework can be applied to partially address the challenges and problems in characterizing and evaluating IIR user studies.

CHAPTER   3

Methodology: Paper Selection and Coding Scheme

Compared to the traditional system-focused IR research, IIR studies often appear to be rather complicated in that they usually involve a series of dynamic user characteristics (e.g., cognitive variation, emotional state, behavioral pattern) and rich contextual features (e.g., task facets, see Li and Belkin, 2008; environments of search interaction, such as home and workplace; task mode, such as mono-tasking and multi-tasking), part of which are fairly difficult to predict or control. Meanwhile, this complexity also creates sizable room and unprecedented opportunities for IR researchers and system designers to personalize users' search interactions (Belkin, 2008; Teevan, Dumais, and Horvitz, 2007, 2010). As it is discussed in previous chapters, a comprehensive, faceted framework of user study can be of help for IIR study design, reporting, and evaluation in multiple streams of research (i.e., understanding user behavior and experience, system/interface features evaluation, meta-evaluation of evaluation metrics).

To obtain a deeper understanding of the state-of-the-art user study practices and develop an up-to-date faceted evaluation framework, we followed Cooper (1989)'s approach and conducted a systematic review on recently published IIR research literature. Cooper's systematic review approach consists of several major steps: (1) state and clarify research problems/focuses (in this case, identify the facets of IIR studies and develop a comprehensive framework to illustrate the role of and, more importantly, the connections between the facets); (2) develop guidelines for collecting literature, especially the criteria for literature inclusion and exclusion; (3) develop a comprehensive search plan for finding literature (in our case, select the most relevant venues where high-quality IIR research are published); (4) develop code form and coding scheme for classifying and characterizing collected literature; (5) code the literature; and (6) synthesize the literature. Since step 1 is already completed in the previous chapters, in this chapter, we will explain steps 2–3 in paper selection (Section 3.1) and discuss steps 4–6 in the coding scheme (Section 3.2).

Overall, in this study, we manually examined 462 IIR user study papers published between 2000 and 2018. Specifically, we focused on the following major venues: ACM SIGIR Conference on Research and Development in Information Retrieval (SIGIR, 2000–2018, n=109), ACM SIGIR Conference on Human Information Interaction and Retrieval (CHIIR, 2016–2018, n=48), ACM Conference on Human Factors in Computing Systems (CHI, 2000–2018, n=126), *Journal of the Association for Information Science and Technology* (*JASIST*, 2010–2018, n=102), *Information Pro-*

cessing and Management (*IP&M*, 2010–2018, n=61), and *ACM Transactions on Information Systems* (*TOIS*, 2010–2018, n=10).

We chose these venues as our sources for paper selection primarily for three reasons.

1. They are major international venues for the publication of research papers on current IIR research problems and advances. Therefore, the IIR research published in these venues can jointly serve as a good representation of the state-of-the-art of user study practices.

2. These venues are relatively strict on study design reporting practices compared to other relevant venues. Thus, user study papers published in these venues are more likely to offer sufficiently detailed information on study design and procedure and hence can serve as appropriate raw materials for developing the scheme of user study.

3. Despite the similarity in broad research problems, different venues focus on different specific topics and approaches and thus can offer diverse perspectives on IIR user study design. Specifically, for example, papers published in SIGIR usually focus more on system-side features (e.g., algorithm, system latency) evaluation, whereas CHIIR community is more interested in understanding user characteristics and behaviors that are manifested in search interactions.

IIR papers presented in CHI community usually address problems related to the role of innovative interface components (e.g., embedded tool and search assistant) in supporting the interaction between human and computing systems. It is worth noting that the growth of IIR research in multiple reputable venues confirms the importance of IIR user studies, and also demonstrates the IR community's acceptance of including users, interacting with information, as one of the major research focuses (Belkin, 2015).

Note that we did not extend the scope of journal paper reviewing to 2000 as we did for all conference venues because we noticed that the majority of the user study papers published in the three journals before 2010 (i.e., *JASIST*, *IP&M*, *TOIS*) reported widely adopted user study procedures and techniques (e.g., survey, semi-structured in-depth interview) which were already extracted from the most recent journal articles and conference papers (especially papers presented in CHIIR). Therefore, including them in paper coding would not add any main facet or lead to any major revision of the faceted framework that emerged from the existing IIR literature. We believe that narrowing down the time frame of journal paper reviewing in this way can help us reduce the unnecessary workload of paper coding without losing any major factors and better focus on the identified facets and factors that were adopted, manipulated, and discussed in a wide range of IIR user studies.

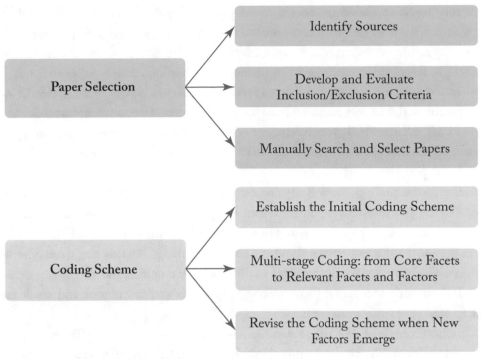

Figure 3.1: Paper selection and coding scheme.

3.1   PAPER SELECTION: SIGIR, CHIIR, CHI, *JASIST*, *IP&M*, AND *TOIS*

The primary purposes of our paper survey are: (1) carefully examine the facets of recent IIR user studies and their combinations in respective research contexts; and (2) develop a faceted evaluation framework which can be applied to a variety of research problems and future meta-evaluation of study design and reporting practices.

With respect to paper selection criteria, this work includes IIR user studies *where researchers conducted user studies (e.g., recruited real participants, designed systems and/or interventions) to evaluate experimental systems and/or examine user behavior and experience in online information seeking.* We did not only select IIR evaluation research, as many other types of human focused user studies also contribute to the understanding of evaluation-related fundamental concepts (e.g., information need, uncertainty, anomalous state of knowledge). Additionally, we excluded user studies where researchers directly employed existing behavioral datasets for evaluation or meta-analysis and provided very limited information about study designs and research contexts.

To ensure the accuracy of including and excluding papers based on our criteria, instead of using keyword searching, we manually reviewed the titles, and abstracts of *all papers published during the time period on the selected venues.* In the cases where the paper types are not clear in the title and abstract, we read the main text until we figured out if the paper actually met our criteria. In terms of the implementation of the paper selection criteria defined above, during the course of paper selection, we carefully examined the methodology section of each paper that was recently published in the selected venues and filtered out the researcher papers that (1) clearly indicated that the experimental data was extracted from existing large-scale datasets and test collections (e.g., TREC, NTCIR, CLEF, AOL search logs), or (2) showed no clear evidence confirming that the authors actually carried out a new user study to collect fresh data on user behavior, evaluation, and/ or interaction experience.

Similar to the findings from Kelly and Sugimoto (2013), during paper selection we found many cases where IIR researchers published multiple papers using one dataset from the same user study. For these user study papers, to avoid repetition and potential bias we only included the one that offers the most sufficient details about the user study design. In this way we can better focus on the diverse facets of user studies reported in different communities, and also obtain more details regarding IIR research topics and focuses, specific methods and techniques, and result reporting styles for faceted user study evaluation.

Overall, we obtained 462 IIR user study papers that jointly cover a wide range of research problems and topics, methods, and findings in the area of IR. In terms of the focuses of the selected venues, while SIGIR has been publishing papers on both the topics of IIR evaluation and understanding user behavior and experience in recent years, the main focus is still on evaluating search system features, such as interface component, search assistant, and underlying ranking algorithms. For example, Singla, White, and Huang (2010) evaluated and compared the performances of different trail-finding algorithms in web search and demonstrated the value of mining and recommending search trails based on users' search logs collected via a widely distributed browser plugin. Wan, Li, and Xiao (2010) developed a multi-document summarization system to automatically extract easy-to-understand English summaries (EUSUM) for non-native readers. They ran a user study to evaluate the novel system and their results indicated that the EUSUM system can produce more useful, understandable summaries for non-native readers than the baseline summarization techniques.

As it is illustrated in these two representative cases, system-evaluation-focused studies published in SIGIR (as well as other reputable IR venues) often start with a practical IR problem and present an innovative system, or a new component of a system, as a solution to the problem highlighted. Then, the role of user study here is to evaluate the system with users and to empirically demonstrate the value of the system in terms of a series of predefined facets or dimensions, such as usefulness, relevance, usability, perceived workload, and effectiveness. Despite this longstanding focus on IR evaluation, there is growing research effort on understanding search behavior and experience within IR community in recent years (e.g., Edwards and Kelly, 2017; Lagun and

Agichtein, 2015; Ong et al., 2017). It is worth noting that the newly opened track of *Human Factors and Interfaces* in SIGIR conference can offer more opportunities for the top-tier IR community to accept more diverse information seeking and search studies that do not entirely focus on the topic of system evaluation.

Compared to SIGIR, CHIIR as a community dedicated to user-centered IR research has offered much room for all three lines of IIR studies. Particularly, more information seeking and search studies are obtaining visibility in CHIIR platform. For instance, He and Yilmaz (2017) characterized users' search tasks emerged in naturalistic settings and discussed the connections among different facets of tasks. This work sheds light on task characteristics in real-life information seeking episodes and can offer useful insights on designing and evaluating task-specific IR systems and recommendations. Wang, Sarkar, and Shah (2018) investigated how people judge the adequacy, accuracy, relevance, and trustworthiness of different types of impersonal and interpersonal information sources and how task type affects individuals' evaluations of information sources. These studies explore different aspects of user and search context (e.g., task) in information seeking and search and thus contribute valuable insights on identifying and characterizing a variety of user-oriented facets of study design.

IIR studies published in CHI mainly cover user behavior research and search interface evaluation. In fact, many of the published papers start with introducing and exploring the hidden problems in search interaction and then focus on the actionable interface design solutions. This approach to developing knowledge on IIR fits well with the HCI community's focus on user interfaces of different types, and also offers more diverse perspectives that largely enriched our understanding on user-centered IR problems. For example, Morris et al. (2018) studied the needs and encountered obstacles of information searchers with dyslexia and demonstrated that factoring readability into search engine ranking and result presentation on interfaces can benefit both dyslexic and non-dyslexic searchers. In this case, the mission of the conducted user study is to build a bridge between users' needs and actionable implications for search interfaces and algorithms design. Vtyurina and Fourney (2018) explored the role of implicit conversational cues (e.g., intonation) in guided task support with virtual assistants and demonstrated that many of user-assistant interaction in a guided task process were initiated from implicit conversational cues rather than from plain, explicit questions. The associated findings generate important implications for detecting triggers and inferring user intents in conversational search interaction. Kim et al. (2017) investigated the diverse Internet search roles of adults in everyday-life information seeking (ELIS) and explained how in-home contextual factors affect search roles and how systems and interfaces can be designed to support the roles of different types.

With respect to the journals (i.e., *JASIST*, *IP&M*, and *TOIS*), they each cover all three streams and major aspects of IIR research (e.g., supporting search tactics, Xie, Joo, and Bennett-Kapusniak, 2017; understanding the role of query auto-completion in search sessions, Smith, Gwizdka, and Feild, 2017; evaluating the behavioral impact of MeSH terms, Liu and Wacholder, 2017; representing user activity pattern in web search, Cole et al., 2015; studying the impacts of domain expertise on search interaction and outcome, Mao et al., 2018). In terms of quantity, during the time period from 2010–2018, *JASIST* has published more user study papers (n=106, especially more papers on understanding and predicting user characteristics) than *IP&M* (n=61) and *TOIS* (n=10). In paper coding, we started with the conference papers as they often report the latest research and methods and cover a large range of user study types.

We built our initial coding schemes based upon the main facets identified in Kelly (2009) as well as some of the representative papers extracted from SIGIR, CHIIR, and CHI. We found that the major facets included in the initial coding scheme can also be applied to characterize most of the IIR research reported in the three journal venues. We continuously revised the coding scheme and added new facets and factors identified from user study papers until we reached a saturation point and finally exhausted all papers in our entire paper collection. More details regarding the paper coding process are reported in the following section.

3.2   CODING SCHEME

To develop the initial coding scheme, we started with 12 basic facets adapted from Kelly (2009) for the initial paper coding. These initial facets and the associated subfacets (provided in parentheses) include: *research focus* (research questions/goals, independent variable(s), dependent variable(s)), *experimental design*, *participants* (sample size, demographics, motivations and incentives), *environment*, *instrument* (e.g., questionnaires, diary, interview, browser plugin, eye-tracker), *behavioral measurements*, *task* (search task, work task), *user interface*, *search collection/corpus*, *ranking algorithm*, *data analysis*, and *results*. These 12 basic facets jointly serve as the root of the tree for a more comprehensive faceted evaluation framework introduced in the following chapter.

We began the coding process using the coding scheme above, and applied it to the collected user study papers. Our coding process started with extracting the research focus of the user study, as it is the fundamental "ground truth" for evaluating user study design and reporting practices. In other words, the goodness-of-user studies should be evaluated based upon their abilities in answering the proposed research questions in the defined research contexts.

After the research foci were clarified, we gradually expanded our coding scheme by extracting values of the other facets and the associated subfacets. During the coding process, we revised and improved our coding framework as we encountered new facets or elements that could not be grouped under any of the existing facets and subfacets. For instance, during the coding and framework revision process, we added a subheading, *answer search task*, under the subfacet search task, aiming to clarify if a search task was answered by participants, or merely served as a context for judging and finding relevant or useful documents. This dimension of task can be easily ignored, yet it may significantly affect the results of studies, as it is clearly related to participants' motivations and cognitive efforts during information searching. Hence, it is critical to take this factor into consideration especially in the studies where task effect is the major research focus.

Similarly, we added the subheading, *do work task*, under the subfacet *work task*, in order to indicate the role of work task (i.e., completed by participants or merely served as a context/problematic situation). The subheading *search task source* was added to clarify if the task was externally assigned or self-generated. For instance, He and Yilmaz (2017) did task analysis based upon user-generated search tasks, whereas Liu et al. (2010, 2019) designed search tasks according to a defined task classification scheme and assigned them to participants in laboratory environment. This factor again is closely related to users' implicit motivations and associated behaviors. Another example is that we included a search assistance tool as a new facet in our framework as we found that there is a growing number of IIR studies examining the effects of assigned non-traditional search assistance tools designed by researchers on users' behaviors and search experience (e.g., Capra et al., 2015; Wan, Li, and Xiao, 2010). To avoid possible confusion, the studies where researchers manipulated traditional, existing search interface element(s) (e.g., query suggestion, search result snippet, SERP size) were differentiated from each other primarily under the facet entitled *search interface element varied* and were coded as "not applicable (N.A.)" under the search assistance tool facet (cf. Kelly and Azzopardi, 2015; Yamamoto and Yamamoto, 2018).

Similar to the approach adopted by Sun and Belkin (2015), in this work the coding process was mainly done by the first author and the coding scheme was discussed by two authors iteratively for continuous revisions and updates. The coding process reached a saturation point where reviewing more papers did not result in any new facet or subfacet. One could argue that the lack of inter-coder agreement measure may weaken the reliability and generalizability of the facet scheme. However, in our case, since the IR research papers are often well structured, the facets, techniques, and components of user studies are usually salient and easy to identify and disambiguate. Hence, our coding process is largely different from the qualitative analyses (e.g., grounded theory approach) on interview transcripts or field observations where the (implicit) meanings behind the text often need to be inferred and even reconstructed (Charmaz, 2014).

Our faceted evaluation framework is presented in the following chapter. Unlike prior relevant works (e.g., Kelly, 2009), our work not only reviews the facets of user study practices (including both design and reporting practices), but also reveals the relationships and combinations between these facets in different research contexts and thereby directly sheds light on the diverse decisions of study design compromise in IIR user studies. Chapter 5 illustrates how the faceted scheme we constructed here can be applied in characterizing and evaluating IIR user studies of different types.

CHAPTER 4

Faceted Framework of IIR User Studies

Faceted approach as a widely used tool in conceptual analysis and library science classification research can help researchers deconstruct a complex concept or entity into several specific, interrelated facets and dimensions and thereby can facilitate theorization, typology development, as well as the associated empirical studies. One of the most relevant faceted frameworks in the area of IIR is Li and Belkin's (2008) faceted classification scheme of task in information seeking and retrieval. This chapter presents the faceted framework which was gradually developed and iteratively revised during the paper coding process, as our response to the very first research goal that we proposed in Chapter 1: develop a faceted framework of user study characterization and evaluation and identify easily ignored user-side facets and factors. To fully address this problem, we first discuss the main facets and the associated subfacets (e.g., research focus, task, system feature) here as they jointly serve as the basis for user study design. Then, we identify a series of easily ignored, under-reported facets that may significantly affect the process and result of user study.

In the following sections, the identified user study facets or dimensions will be discussed in detail and be illustrated with the associated examples or representative user studies from selected venues. The final version of faceted user study framework is shown in Figure 4.1, and will be explained piece by piece in this chapter. Built upon the collection of recently published IIR user studies from a variety of top venues, our faceted framework can offer a comprehensive picture of the-state-of-the-art user study practice and facilitate faceted analysis (e.g., generating standard metadata of user studies for summarization, comparative analysis, and evaluation).

4.1 STRUCTURE OF THE FACETED FRAMEWORK

Despite the uniqueness of every user study (especially in terms of the specific techniques and system features), it is still possible and also critical for researchers to extract main common facets and subfacets from a pool of specific IIR user studies and to figure out how these facets are defined, designed, and manipulated according to the nature of the proposed research problems and goals. We believe that a comprehensive, faceted framework of user study can serve as a checklist for IIR researchers to reflect on when they design, report, and evaluate various user studies. Based on our qualitative coding, iterative discussion and continuous revision of the coding scheme, we developed a faceted framework of IIR user study which consists of nine *main facets*: (1) the root or starting

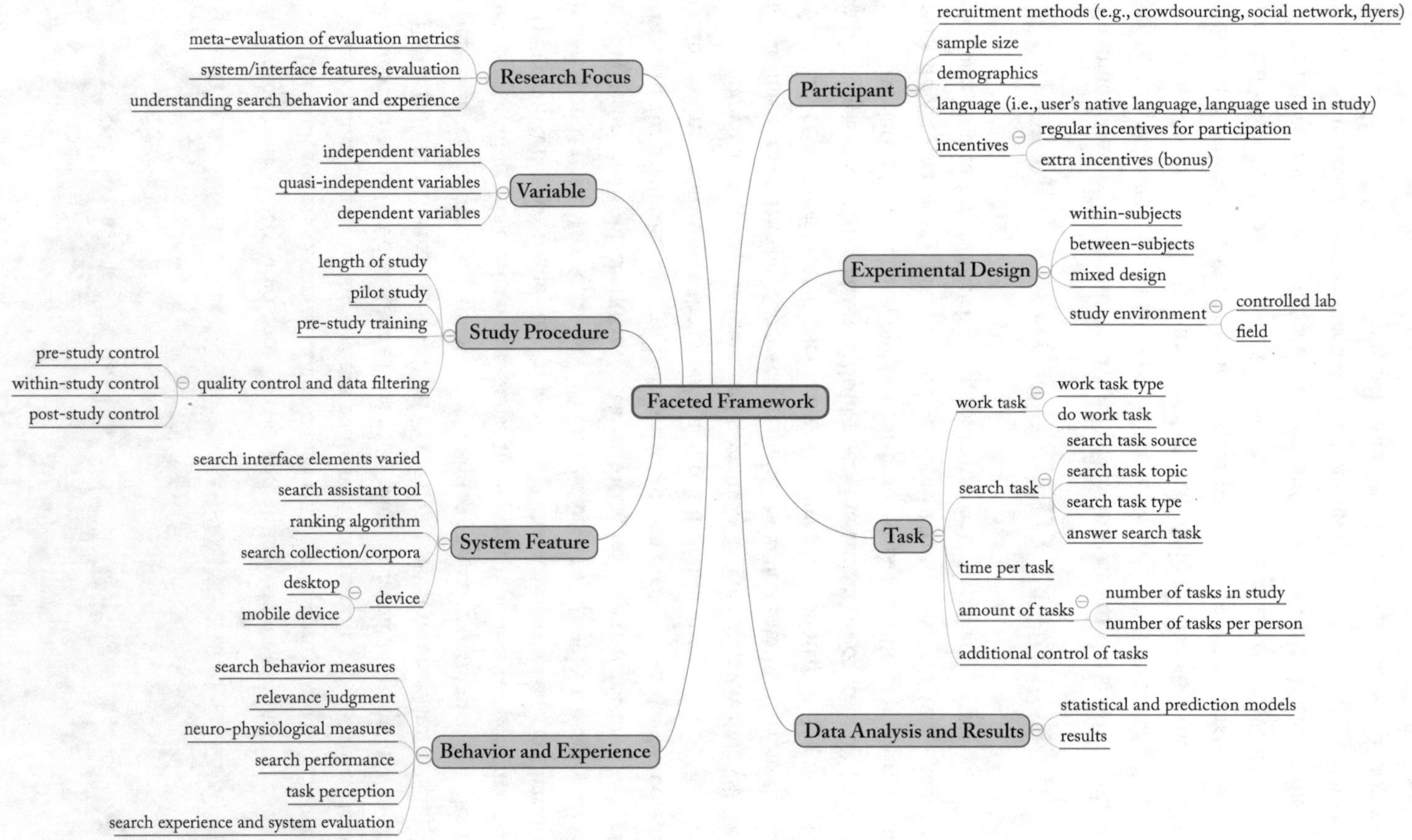

Figure 4.1: Faceted evaluation framework of interactive IR user studies.

facets of a user study: *research focus and variable*; (2) main facets and factors to be manipulated: *participant*, *task*, and *system feature*; (3) study procedure facets: *study procedure* and *experimental design*; and (4) measurement and analysis facet: *behavior and experience*, *data analysis, and results*.

Among these four categories of main facets, research focus and variables are the *root facets* and default items of user study design and fundamentally determine other the manipulation of other main facets (e.g., participant, task type, system and interface features to be varied). Once the specific variables and associated factors are decided, the study procedure and experimental design (if applicable) can also be determined and unfolded accordingly. Then, based on the specific research problems, variables defined, and data collection techniques, researchers need to decide the specific models and methods for data analysis and consider: (1) if the data analysis technique fits well with the whole research design and procedure; and (2) to what extent the adopted methods and models of analysis can (at least partially) address the limitations caused by the decisions made in study procedure design. For example, a user-centered search behavior research may involve multiple independent variables that come from different levels (e.g., user level, task and session levels, query segment level). Under this circumstance, applying multi-level or hierarchical linear model can help clarify the effects caused by the variables from different levels in causal inference and thereby mitigate the negative influence caused by the decisions and compromises in user study design. The connections among main facets discussed above are illustrated in Figure 4.2. The main facets and associated subfacets will be explained in detail in the following subsections.

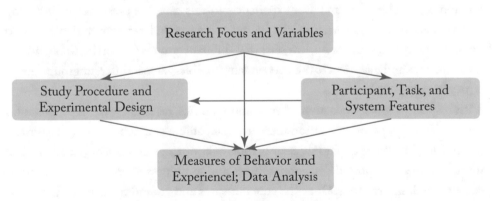

Figure 4.2: Connections among different categories of user study facets.

4.1.1   RESEARCH FOCUS AND VARIABLES

According to the divergent research focuses, IIR user studies can be roughly classified into three categories: (1) understanding user behavior and experience; (2) system or interface features evaluation; and (3) meta-evaluation of evaluation metrics. Given the research focus and associated research questions, researchers have to define corresponding variables as a preparation for user study design, subsequent data analysis (e.g., statistical modeling) and result presentation. This is part of the basic, default phase of user study design and will fundamentally define a majority of facet values (e.g., task type, experimental system, participant features). For example, in Ong et al.'s (2017) exploration on the impacts of information scent levels and patterns on search behavior, SERP type can be considered as the core independent variable as it was intentionally manipulated to produce varying information scent levels and patterns. Also, search behavioral measures (e.g., query reformulation, dwell time on pages of different types, clicking behavior) in this case were considered as dependent variables and incorporated into statistical models. Then, to answer the proposed research questions, a user study was designed around these fundamental cornerstones and a series of design decisions (and compromises) were made.

Similarly, researchers focusing on system and interface evaluations often manipulate system and/or interface feature(s) and see if the variation(s) in these features lead to any statistically significant difference in search performance (e.g., higher precision or recall in search; improved performance in task completion) and search interaction experience (e.g., lower workload, higher level of search satisfaction). For instance, Ruotsalo et al. (2018) introduced an innovative assistant tool for search interaction called *Interactive Intent Modeling,* which can model a user's evolving search intents and visualize them as keywords for search interaction. While doing system evaluation, the researchers employed a variety of search performance measures and found that the intent modeling and visualization can significantly improve retrieval effectiveness, users' task performance, breadth of information comprehension, and user experience. In this case, the presentation and adoption of new intent modeling and visualization can be defined as an independent variable as researchers directly manipulated the interaction interface for different groups of participants and compared search performances and experiences (i.e., dependent variables) across different groups (i.e., baseline group vs. treatment group).

With respect to meta-evaluation of evaluation metrics, researchers often propose and evaluate a series of newly proposed evaluation measures (i.e., online search behavioral measures, such as querying behavior, browsing and result examination behavior, eye movement pattern and attention distribution; offline self-reported data, annotations, and usefulness judgments) that capture different aspects of search interactions. Once the core measures and ground truth are defined, researchers usually conduct the meta-evaluation mainly through two ways: (1) examining the correlations between these measures and predefined ground truth (e.g., query-level satisfaction and session-level satisfaction; relevance judgment; search success) (e.g., Chen et al., 2017); and (2) investigating the predicative power of the model built upon new evaluation metrics/features in predicting predefined ground truth value (e.g., Liu et al., 2018).

In summary, clearly defining independent and dependent variables (i.e., the associated concepts, operational definitions, as well as the hypotheses, if applicable) are the default "step one" for user study design and are obviously crucial for most of the IIR research as well as information science research in general. However, clean, manipulatable independent variable at the operationalization level is not always available in all research contexts. In many experimental designs, it is very difficult, if not entirely impossible, to reasonably manipulate some of the variables or factors of interest (especially the factors related to user characteristics and perceptions) due to the nature of these variables as well as the unpredictable impact from various contextual factors. Therefore, as an alternative option, many IIR researchers choose to include *quasi-independent variables* in their user study designs and modeling.

Quasi-independent variables are often associated with individual traits and may be treated as statistically independent but are not subject to random assignment and direct manipulation, as are independent variables (Kelly, 2009). Since many user characteristics cannot be directly manipulated or randomly assigned (e.g., task familiarity, topic knowledge, domain knowledge, perceived task difficulty) through any special design in recruitments, they are often represented by quasi-independent variables in statistical models. For instance, Zhang et al. (2015) studied the effect of users' domain knowledge on their search behaviors and adopted participants' self-reported level of domain knowledge in building statistical and prediction models. In this example, the level of domain knowledge was treated as independent in the regression models. However, as a quasi-independent variable, participants' domain knowledge was not subject to any form of random assignment or predetermined manipulation in the user study design. Consequently, the actual distribution of different domain knowledge levels was not fully controlled by the researchers.

Similarly, Liu et al. (2010) employed a series of self-reported task features and user characteristics (e.g., task difficulty, topic knowledge) and investigated how these quasi-independent variables affect users' querying behavior, browsing and result examination strategies, and eye movements in task-based search sessions. Aula, Khan, and Guan (2010) studied how users' search tactics vary across different levels of (self-reported) task difficulty. Again, in these examples, quasi-independent variables were measured mainly through self-reported metrics (e.g., 5-point or 7-point Likert Scales) and were not directly designed or manipulated by researchers. Thus, compared to independent variables (e.g., task type, task product, task goal, system/interface features), quasi-independent variables are often more difficult to control and are subject to the impacts caused by a variety of even unknown contextual factors. This is one of the reasons why it is critical to control seemingly irrelevant contextual variables and hidden factors in data analyses when quasi-independent variable(s) are involved in user study design.

4.1.2   PARTICIPANT AND TASK

In IIR user studies (especially in the research focusing on understanding user behavior and experience), participant and task are two of the central facets that fundamentally determine the scope and direction of data collection process (e.g., what type of behavioral data can be collected, from whom should we collect data, what is the nature of the tasks that contextualize participants' interactions with search systems). As is shown in Figure 4.1, we identified a series of subfacets under these two facets and found that these two main facets and the associated subfacets not only affect the study procedure, but also partially decide the quality of data collected, the reliability of statistical results, as well as the generalizability of the findings emerged from the empirical evidences. This subsection explains the two main facets and the related subfacets in detail with examples from the research paper collection.

Participant recruitment is the starting point of user study procedure and determines the source of available data (e.g., search behavioral data, self-reported and neuro-physiological data on interaction experience, search evaluation data). Different recruitment methods are often associated with different experimental setups. From our collection of user study papers, we summarized two main recruitment approaches: (1) widely used small-scale user study recruitment methods, such as flyers, in-class recruitment, personal social networks, and internal mailing lists; and (2) large-scale crowdsourcing techniques, such as recruitment within certain institutions (e.g., Microsoft's large-scale user studies) or via professional crowdsourcing and survey platforms (e.g., Amazon Mechanical Turk, SurveyMonkey). In small-scale user studies, researchers usually expect high commitment from participants and ask them to engage in relatively complex tasks (e.g., complex search task and work task, relevance and usefulness judgments, post-search in-depth interview) that need to be carried out through specific experimental systems and/or within certain controlled lab settings. With a variety of predefined constraints and conditions, researchers are more likely to collect a variety of more detailed, reliable data on users' search interactions, cognition, and experience.

Let us examine a couple of examples. Cole et al. (2013) invited participants to complete predefined search tasks in their controlled lab and collected data on their search interactions. In this case, researchers had a relatively nice control over a series of contextual factors (e.g., task type, task topic, search system and interface) and successfully collected several types of data on users' search interactions, including search behavioral data, eye movement data, and qualitative data regarding search experience and obstacles from post-search interview transcripts. Moshfeghi, Triantafillou, and Pollick (2016) conducted an fMRI study on information needs and demonstrated that users' knowledge states (i.e., information need, anomalous state of knowledge) can be inferred from the activities of certain neuro-physiological signals. Apparently, at least part of the data collected in these small-scale user studies would not be available if the participants were recruited and participated in the study via crowdsourcing platform.

When we look at the limitations, the recruitment methods used in small-scale (often lab-based) user studies are inefficient, time consuming, and expensive. To reduce the cost and expedite participant recruitment and data collection process, many researchers in research institutions tend to adopt convenience sampling methods and recruit students on campus as their participants. However, only studying information seeking and search behaviors of students from the same campus may result in the lack of variation in participants' knowledge background and eventually limits the generalizability of the findings. Hence, for small-scale user studies, researchers have to go beyond students and universities and to investigate non-student users' search interactions in naturalistic settings.

Compared to small-scale recruitment methods, a crowdsourcing platform is more efficient for participant recruitment in that (1) it can easily recruitment large amounts of participants that meet certain predefined requirements (e.g., education level, language, experience and performance in previous studies); and (2) researchers do not need to directly engage in the recruitment process or worry about space and time constraints. Participants can be automatically recruited via crowdsourcing tools in different time zones when researchers are sleeping (Kittur, Chi, and Suh, 2008). For example, Zhang et al. (2014) explored the multidimensionality of document relevance and collected human relevance judgment data via Amazon Mechanical Turk. Five hundred and two participants were recruited from the crowdsourcing platform and provided rich relevance judgment data for researchers to conduct both Exploratory Factor Analysis and Confirmatory Factor Analysis.

In contrast to the crowdsourcing research, in small-scale user studies, IIR researchers (including the authors) often find it difficult to recruit even more than forty participants within several months. Note that some of the small-scale user studies do have their own recruitment and registration systems that allow participants to sign up for the study by themselves. However, in these situations, researchers still need to actively advocate their study through different channels and the recruitment efficiency is usually quite low compared to crowdsourcing studies.

Despite the advantages discussed above, crowdsourcing recruitment has limitations. First, researchers often find it challenging to control the quality of data collected through crowdsourcing platform as participants need to complete the entire study "in the wild" and the incentives/payments often turn out to be the only reason that motivates people to participate (in other words, researchers cannot ensure that participants are really paying attention to the tasks and assignments in their studies). To address this issue, many researchers set up several filters in their task and survey (e.g., timer, trap questions) to help them filter out low-quality data before conducting analysis. Second, with respect to the associated study procedure, it is difficult for researchers to incorporate complex tasks (involving many steps and a variety of actions) into crowdsourcing study settings and also to expect good-quality data automatically come out from the study.

Given these limitations, many user study researchers have developed multiple approaches to increase participants' engagement and curiosity in crowdsourcing studies in order to improve data quality (Law et al., 2016; Zhao and Zhu, 2014).

Sample size is another critical subfacet as it is highly relevant to the validity of statistical results and the associated conclusions. On the reader's side, sample size is also one of the important dimensions based upon which reviewers judge the quality of a given piece of IIR user research. Sakai (2016) discussed the importance of power analysis in IR study (especially in statistical significance tests) and argued that researchers need to determine an appropriate sample size according to the study setup (e.g., number of separate groups) and specific analysis methods adopted (e.g., parametric methods vs. nonparametric methods) and to avoid both overpowered and underpowered situations in statistical modeling. In addition to sample size and recruitment methods, demographic characteristics (e.g., gender and age composition, educational background, occupation) as important user characteristics are also frequently reported in the form of descriptive statistics in IIR research papers.

Task design is a major component of many IIR user study design as it contextualizes users' interactions with search systems. In most task-based IR studies, researchers usually assign predefined search tasks to participants and ask them to search for information that is relevant to the task topic or useful for addressing the tasks. There are also a few field studies where researchers study the characteristics and distributions of users' self-reported, authentic tasks of different types (e.g., He and Yilmaz, 2017). Note that we included *search task source* as a subfacet in the framework because the sources of tasks may significantly affect users' motivations, search strategies, and performances in task-based search sessions.

To deconstruct tasks and represent different aspects of them in empirical studies, task features and facets are often measured via separate independent variables in user-centered IR research (e.g., Liu et al., 2010; Zhang et al., 2015). According to Li and Belkin (2008), a task (i.e., work task, information seeking and search task) can be deconstructed into several facets and dimensions (e.g., task product, task goal, task stage, time length, urgency) that can be operationalized as different variables. In addition, work task and search task should be treated as different levels of the entire task context because work task as a broader context often motivates subjects to engage in a series of information seeking and search tasks and to interact with search systems (Byström and Hansen, 2005; Li, 2009; Li and Belkin, 2010). Therefore, defining task context in IIR user study not only involves the design of specific search tasks, but also includes the construction of associated work tasks or search scenarios as the backgrounds of the search tasks at hand (cf. Borlund, 2016; Mitsui et al., 2017). Unfortunately, many of the recently published IIR user studies merely defined and presented search tasks to participants and left out the related work task or search scenario descriptions, resulting in the lack of broader contexts or "cover stories" as well as the realism of natural search activities.

In addition to Li and Belkin (2008)'s faceted scheme, researchers have also proposed some other task typologies that focus on one of the core aspects or facets of task context. For example, Kelly et al. (2015) developed a cognitive complexity framework to characterize tasks of different types and demonstrated that tasks of varying complexity can lead to different web search strategies. Capra et al. (2018) focused on the factors affecting task prior determinability and indicated that manipulating the dimensions and information items of tasks in different ways result in statistically significant differences in some aspects of search behaviors and outcomes. These typologies and the associated empirical works enhanced our understanding of certain aspects of task and shed lights on the design and manipulation of task features in IIR user studies.

4.1.3   SYSTEM FEATURE

Designing and manipulating system features often turns out to be a critical step in many IIR user studies, especially in user-oriented IR evaluation research. As it is discussed in Chapter 2, some researchers choose to manipulate existing system or interface features (e.g., SERP size, query term suggestion) for system evaluation, whereas other researchers design new features, affordances, and search assistant tools (e.g., search trail tool, chatbot) in order to create and observe new interaction patterns. Yamamoto and Yamamoto (2018) sought to promote critical thinking in the search process via query priming and their results demonstrated that using query suggestions can facilitate searchers' critical thinking and analysis and thereby improve their search performances in certain types of search tasks. In this case, the researchers manipulated a widely-adopted existing system feature (i.e., query term suggestions) and evaluated various versions of the feature or affordance with users based on their interactive behaviors and performances. One of the prominent advantages of using existing, widely applied system and interface feature(s) is that participants usually do not need to take too much time and efforts to practice and get familiar with the manipulated version of the system (because the manipulated feature here is not entirely new). Therefore, compared to introducing brand new features and conducting IR system evaluation, it might be much easier for researchers to elicit natural search behavior and responses from participants with this type of study settings.

Differing from Yamamoto and Yamamoto (2018), some user studies designed and evaluated new system or interface features in search interactions. For instance, Ruotsalo et al. (2018) designed an innovative assistant tool (i.e., interactive intent modeling) and visualized user intents using keywords for supporting search interactions. Then, the researchers evaluated the new system with a between-subject user study design (i.e., experimental system group versus baseline group) and demonstrated that mining, predicting, and visualizing search intents can effectively facilitate users' query formulations and thereby improve their search performance and overall experience. Similarly, Bateman, Teevan, and White (2012) created and assessed a new tool named *Search Dashboard* that provides a useful interface for users to reflect on multiple aspects of their own search strategies (e.g., query formulation, click and result examination). Their research demonstrated that reflecting on personal search behavior can be beneficial to users as it changes their views and understanding of their own search tactics and what can be accomplished with the current search system. Nicholson et al. (2014) reported a user-centered evaluation of *Panopticon*, a video surrogate system as a support search tool for finding information within video lectures. Using the standard video player (YouTube) as the baseline to compare with in evaluation, the study indicated that their new search support tool can significantly expedite information finding within the lecture videos. Regarding the system features "behind the scenes," Syed and Collins-Thompson (2017) proposed novel retrieval algorithms that can generate personalized search results tailored to a variety of human learning goals and assessed the effectiveness of the innovative retrieval and ranking algorithms in improving participants' word-learning outcomes.

User studies that manipulate system and/or interface features can offer empirical basis for IIR system evaluation and also shed light on the development of search systems and the design of user interfaces in various settings (e.g., home setting, workplace, public and school libraries). In addition to these subfacets, system features also involve other important aspects, such as the devices on which a search system can operate (e.g., desktop computer, tablet, smartphones), test collections and corpora. Particularly, some IIR research focus on the differences in user search behavior across different types of devices and suggest that users often adjust their search strategies according to some specific interface features (e.g., search result representation, SERP size, information scent level) of the systems running on different devices (e.g., Harvey and Pointon, 2017; Ong et al., 2017; Song et al., 2013). These studies can provide actionable design implications for system and interface designers and facilitate user-centered evaluations of personalized search systems.

4.1.4   STUDY PROCEDURE AND EXPERIMENTAL DESIGN

As Figure 4.2 illustrates, the procedure of an IIR user study is largely affected by the proposed research questions, externally assigned or self-generated task types, user characteristics, as well as the system and interface features manipulated or created by researchers. Based on the proposed research questions and the related variables, researchers need to decide other components and steps of the user study and to figure out the design decisions and compromises they have to make in order to properly address the research problems with available resources.

Due to the nature of different research questions, some of the user studies adapted experimental design from psychology and applied the associated methods in studying the search behaviors of users with different characteristics and in evaluating innovative search systems. The treatments in IIR user studies often involve the main facet(s) or core factors, such as task facet and task type (e.g., factual task vs. intellectual task), user group (e.g., expert group vs. novice group), and system features (e.g., experimental system group vs. baseline system group). To create a suitable, reliable experimental setting, researchers have to not only design and refine the treatment condition(s), but also think carefully about how to define a reasonable baseline condition. Thus, the justification of a user study (especially experimental) design should detailedly describe and explain both the treatment part and baseline part. On top of that, researchers also have the obligation to come up with a reasonable ground truth if the user study involves user-centered evaluation of any kind, such as interface evaluation, new search tool evaluation, and ranking algorithm evaluation.

In addition to the basic components discussed above, a user study researcher also needs to adjust the values of other subfacets associated with the study procedure and experimental design. For instance, as a preparation work for many user studies, pilot study and pre-study training or tutorial should be properly reported and discussed in user study papers. These *pre-study parts* are critical for user study evaluation especially in the cases where participants are asked to interact with entirely new system features or a search interface and thus need more time to get familiarized with it so that they can interact with the search system in a more natural manner. In addition to these two pre-study components, researchers also need to reflect on other dimensions of user studies, such as the length of study (balancing data richness and user fatigue), methods of data quality control at different stages of user study (i.e., pre-study control in participant recruitment, within-study control, post-study control and data filtering), types of experimental design (i.e., within-subject design, between-subject design, mixed design), and overall study environment (e.g., field/naturalistic settings and controlled lab settings). The decisions and choices made under each of these facets all represent different design decisions made in study design. The "collaboration" among these facets can jointly affect the level of richness of the data collected as well as the quality and reliability of the final results. For instance, some researchers choose to conduct studies in field settings instead of controlled laboratory environments may be because addressing the identified research problem(s) requires researcher to extract natural tasks and to elicit natural search strategies and responses as much as possible (e.g., He and Yilmaz, 2017). At the same time, however, as a "price" of this choice, some types of control and support over the search context may become unavailable (e.g., task type, real-time interventions). Another example is about the facet of experimental design. In the IIR evaluation studies in which multiple tasks and/or systems are involved, adopting between-subject design can help avoid possible learning effects, which is very likely to happen in the studies that employ within-subjects design. Meanwhile, however, to facilitate model building and to maintain the required statistical power in significance tests, researchers using between-subjects design have to recruit more participants (for avoiding underpowered situations), which is often difficult to achieve for offline recruitments. In addition to these two types of experimental design, adopting mixed design may allow researchers to apply and investigate more complicated combinations of different facet values in various study settings (e.g., the combination between task type and interface feature). Nevertheless, researchers still need to be mindful of the limitations from both sides.

Study procedure and experimental design are two of the main facets that shape the ways in which multiple facets and variables discussed above interact with each other and jointly decide the direction and quality of data collection and analyses. In other words, these two facets jointly serve as the bridge connecting the input part (e.g., task context design, population selection and participant recruitment, manipulation and design of system features) and the output part (e.g., search behavior and experience measures, results) of IIR user studies. Therefore, through digging into the details of user study procedure and experimental settings, researchers can better detect, understand, and explain study design decisions and compromises made in terms of a variety of facets and associated subfacets.

4.1.5   USER BEHAVIOR, EXPERIENCE, DATA ANALYSIS, AND RESULTS

To capture and evaluate the products of user studies, researchers have developed a variety of user behavioral, performance, and experience measures, including both online measures collected within search sessions and offline measures consisting of user annotations, document relevance and usefulness judgments, and other self-reported metrics (e.g., NASA Task Load Index, user engagement indicators). To extract useful insights and actionable implications from the empirical evidence emerged from user studies, researchers also have to feed raw data into mathematical models and wait for the results on the output side. As is illustrated in Figures 4.1 and 4.2, the adoption of behavioral measures and analytical models is often determined based upon the research problems identified as well as the variables and associated main facets defined in user study design.

The metric of user behaviors and interaction experiences (e.g., satisfaction, cognitive load, frustration) is a fundamental aspect of the user studies that aim at understanding users and applying user-centered approach in search systems design and evaluation. With respect to user behaviors, past user studies have explored various possible approaches to measuring multiple components of information seeking and search episodes, such as querying (e.g., query formulation and re-formulation, use of query suggestion, query diversity and complexity), browsing (e.g., dwell time on SERP and landing/content pages), and result examination behavior (e.g., clicks, scrolls, mouse hovering). In addition, researchers also employed offline user judgments (e.g., usefulness and relevance judgment), annotations, and performance measures (e.g., average precision, normalized discounted cumulative gain in search result examination) and evaluated the usefulness of these metrics in IR system evaluation against a series of user-centered ground truth measures (e.g., satisfaction). Chen et al. (2017) provides a summary of existing online and offline behavioral metrics and compared the usefulness and effectiveness of these distinct measures in a user-centered system evaluation. Aside from the explicit search behaviors, performances, and user annotations, some researchers have also explored the possibility of measuring users' cognitive and affective variations and examined the extent to which neuro-physiological measures of different types (e.g., eye movement, pupil size, heart rate, skin conductance rate, EEG and fMRI signals) are associated with traditional behavioral and experience measures (e.g., Cole et al., 2013; Edwards and Kelly, 2017; Eickhoff, Dungs, and Tran, 2015; Eugster et al., 2014; Gwizdka and Zhang, 2015; Moshfeghi, Triantafillou, and Pollick, 2016). In IIR user studies, the behavioral and interaction experience measures discussed above have served as useful sensors for detecting the features and behavioral patterns of users' search interactions. Combining these "behavioral pixels" in modeling, we can obtain a relatively comprehensive picture about how users' interaction with search systems in tasks of different types and how they assess the effectiveness of the system as well as their own search experience in different contexts.

In addition to data collection and measures, data analyses and result presentation methods are also determined by the research questions proposed at the beginning of many user studies. Given the nature of the research problems and goals (e.g., examining the correlation between different behaviors, inferring and predicting subsequent behavior and experience, evaluating a new system or search interface feature with users), researchers have to decide the most appropriate statistics and models (e.g., parametric and nonparametric correlation analysis, linear and nonlinear regression models, machine learning techniques) in order to fully exploit the potential of the data collected via user studies and properly answer research questions with relevant empirical evidences. More detailed discussions regarding the connections between research focus, core components of study procedures, and data analyses will be presented in Chapter 5.

4.1.6   EXAMPLE OF FACETED ANNOTATION

The previous subsections explain the main facets respectively using recently published, the-state-of-the-art IIR user studies as examples. To further illustrate our faceted framework, this subsection presents a representative example of user studies (Bron et al. 2013), and shows how different facets, dimensions, and factors of this study are annotated within our framework. Two more examples about other types of IIR user studies are presented in the Appendix.

User Study Example: Bron et al. (2013)

Research Focus and Variables

[**Research Focus**] IIR evaluation: evaluating interface feature; [**Keywords** (directly extracted from the paper)] search interface preferences, search behavior aggregated search, multi-session search tasks; [**Independent Variable**] interface (tabbed or blended), task; [**Dependent Variable**] mouse hover, search moves (paginate, bookmark, filter, change tab, querying, view documents, bookmark delete, unique queries);

Participant

[**Recruitment**] longitudinal study: recruiting students from a course (for suitable work task); controlled lab study: 42 students recruited on campus; [**Controlled lab**] Yes; [**Field/ Large-scale**] Yes; [**Sample Size**] longitudinal study: 25 participants; lab study: 42 participants (2 filtered); [**Gender Composition**] longitudinal study: 12 males and 13 females. lab study: 12 males, 30 females. [**Participant Occupation**] student; [**Age**] longitudinal study: median = 23; lab study: median = 19; [**Education Background/Level**] longitudinal study: postgraduate level in the area of media studies; lab study: undergraduate students; [**Participants' Native Language(s)**] no information; [**Language Used in Study**] English; [**Regular Incentives**] longitudinal study: availability of unique sources. Lab study: no information. [**Extra Incentives/Bonus**] no information; [**Length of Study**] longitudinal study: 4 weeks; lab study: 1.5 h.

Task

[**Task Source**] longitudinal study: assigned work task in class (i.e., a writing project); lab study: no information; [**Search Task Type**] longitudinal study: user-generated search tasks based on the given writing project (work task); lab study: factual amorphous and factual specific tasks; [**Search Task Topic**] longitudinal study: in historical context of the 1950s or 1920s, explain the emanicipatory role of a famous female television/film personality. lab study: no information; [**Number of Tasks**] longitudinal study: 1 work task; lab study: 6 search tasks; [**Number of tasks/Person**] longitudinal study: 1 work task; lab study: 3 search tasks; [**Time Length/Task**] longitudinal study: 4 weeks; lab study: 10 min; [**Work Task Type**] intellectual amorphous task; [**Did Work Task**] longitudinal study: Yes; [**Answer Search Task**] lab study: N.A. [**Evaluation Task**] lab study: collect at least 5 items deemed to be relevant for each task.

Study Procedure and Experimental Design

[**Task/Session Feature Controlled**] lab study: task order was fixed; [**Task Rotation**] no information; [**Pilot Study**] no information; [**Pre-study Training**] lab session: each occasion of the study started with a brief introduction to the whole research project and a viewing of a 5-min tutorial video explaining the use of the experimental search displays. [**Actual Task Completion Time**] no information; [**Quality Control/Data Filtering Criteria**] lab study: for two of the subjects a technical failure prevented recording the pre-experiment questionnaire data, and hence their data were excluded from further analysis. [**Experimental Design**] longitudinal study: no clear intervention; lab study: mixed design.

System Features

[**Study Interface Element Varied**] blended or tabbed; [**Other System/Context Feature Varied**] N.A.; [**Study Apparatus**] desktop computer; [**Search Collection/Corpus**] six collections from several archives and library materials; [**Ranking Algorithm**] BM25; [**non-traditional IR System Assistance Tool**] blended and tabbed interfaces.

Behavioral and Search Experience Measures

[**Search Behavior Measures**] longitudinal study: mouse hover; lab study: search moves (paginate, bookmark, filter, change tab, queries, view documents, delete bookmark, unique queries); [**Instrument for Collecting Search Behavioral Data**] experimental system; [**Relevance Judgment**] lab study: participants evaluated documents and collected at least 5 relevant items; [**Instrument for Collecting User Judgment**] experimental system; [**Search and System Performance Measures**] N.A.; [**Neuro-physiological Measures**] N.A.; [**Instruments for Capturing Neuro-physiological Measures**] N.A.; [**Offline In-**

formation Seeking Behavior] N.A.; [**Other Information Behavior**] N.A.; [**Data Analysis Method**] Mann-Whitney U test and Kruskal Wallis H test; [**Qualitative Analysis**] in longitudinal study, participants were asked about their motivations of using blended and tabbed interfaces in open question survey as well as post-task 15 min focus group interview. The qualitative data were analyzed and incorporated in result presentation and discussion; [**Level of Analysis**] task level; [**Task-independent Measures**] longitudinal study: pre-task questionnaire asking about levels of experience in general computer use and using online search tools; lab study: pre-search questionnaire collecting demographic information and information about prior search experience; [**Task/Session Perception Measures**] lab study: pre-search questionnaire: prior knowledge about task topic; post-search questionnaire: topic difficulty; [**Search Experience and System Evaluation Measures**] longitudinal study: open question survey and post-task focus group discussion: motivations of using blended and tabbed interfaces; lab study: post search questionnaire asking about perceived usability of the display and the search effectiveness of the display. After the final task: post-experiment questionnaire asking participants to order the displays by preference.

Data Analysis and Results

[**Statistical Test Assumption Check Reported**] Yes; [**Results**] 1. Longitudinal study: while a tabbed display is used more than a blended display, subjects repeatedly switch between displays during search. Use of the tabbed display was motivated by a need to zoom in on a specific information source, while the blended display was adopted to explore available material across sources whenever the user's information need changes. 2. Lab study: a stable information need over multiple sub-tasks negatively influenced perceived usability of the blended displays, while no clear influence was found when the information need changes. [**Effect Size**] no information.

4.2   UNDER-REPORTED FACETS AND FACTORS

In experimental studies, results and findings can be affected in both expected (i.e., affected by designed interventions and recognized research limitations) and unexpected (i.e., influenced by ignored factors and study design components) ways. In this subsection, we highlight the factors and facets that are: (1) under-reported (i.e., reported by less than 50% of the user studies examined) and may significantly affect study results; and (2) can be applied in most of the user study types. Figure 4.3 summarizes these facets and factors that were overlooked by most of the recently published IIR user studies. To illustrate the under-reported facets, this section follows Sakai's (2016) reference practice and uses several examples selected from past user studies.

Participant Native language Incentives (both regular and extra bonus)	**Procedure** Pilot study Pre-study training Quality control and data filtering Length of study	**Task** Do work task Answer search task

Figure 4.3: Under-reported facets and factors.

With respect to participants, around 50% of the studies did not report information concerning participants' English proficiency when all the materials (e.g., documents, instructions, questionnaires) were in English. As a result, we are not sure whether language issues caused any noticeable impact on users' search behavior, relevance judgment, and cognitive efforts, especially in complex, intellectual, information-intensive tasks. For instance, in a SIGIR2017 paper (DOI: 10.1145/3077136.3080829), besides the different types of information visualizations as treatments, participants' language proficiency may also significantly affect their search behaviors in knowledge seeking tasks. Since plenty of the evaluation measures involve users' language processing (e.g., SERP examination, relevance and usefulness judgments, query formulation and reformulation, answering questions asked in task descriptions), we should take this factor into account and employ a reasonable, generalizable measure of it when designing and evaluating IIR user studies.

In terms of study procedure, there are four under-reported factors: length of study, pilot study, pre-study training, quality control, and data filtering.

Length of study is a critical aspect of study procedure and needs to be considered in the evaluation of task loads and user fatigue. In a lengthy search session, users' search strategies and performance may vary significantly across different stages of the search process.

Pilot study is useful especially in terms of estimating the time length of a study as well as identifying potential problems with the instruments, protocols, and instructions (Kelly, 2009). For instance, in a SIGIR2014 paper (DOI: 10.1145/2600428.2609633), researchers conducted a pilot study and found that it is necessary to include task description in the system interface for effectively manipulating search task context. In another example (SIGIR2016, DOI: 10.1145/2911451.2911507), task modifications were made based on the findings from a pilot study. With effective pilot studies, many potential issues in data collection and study procedure can be prevented before the "formal studies" are carried out. Note that pilot tests/studies are different from feasibility tests in that pilot studies are supposed to tell researchers not only if all devices, techniques, and systems are working (which are the main focuses on feasibility tests), but also the types of data they should expect to get (in other words, whether they can obtain the right kind of data they hope to collect with the study procedure and methods at hand).

Pre-study training (e.g., training task, video-based instructions or onsite tutorials) is often included in user study procedure for familiarizing users with the experimental systems and study contexts. This is an important step in the user studies where new experimental systems, interfaces, or contexts are introduced and implemented. For instance, in a SIGIR2017 research (DOI: 10.1145/3077136.3080770), pre-study training information is important for readers to understand how the participants gradually got familiar with different information seeking contexts and how this change in familiarity could affect the final results. Not conducting or reporting pre-study training information may cast doubt on the true effect of the system features on interaction patterns and search experiences, especially in the initial stage of search as the estimated effect may be contaminated by participants' unfamiliarity with the assigned system(s) and/or task(s).

Quality control refers to the design practices in addition to the regular controls (e.g., task type, search interface, search collection) for ensuring the quality of the dataset. According to the examined user studies, we noticed that quality control could be done at different stages: (1) pre-study control: e.g., only recruit native English speakers to exclude the effect of English fluency (SIGIR2017, DOI: 10.1145/3077136.3080840); (2) within-study control: e.g., employ similar designs for both treatment and control SERP groups in within-subjects design to ensure that participants did not notice the intervention (SIGIR2015, DOI: 10.1145/2766462.2767714); and (3) post-study control: e.g., filter out the data from low-quality sessions, exclude the responses which were generated in a very short period of time (SIGIR2014, DOI: 10.1145/2600428.2609566). These quality control practices and reports can help to some extent guarantee the quality of data and thus should be considered when evaluating the validity and reliability of user study results and conclusions.

Task is one of the central components in IIR research. While increased research attention has been devoted to task in the last ten years, most of the past studies focused on a very limited set of facets (e.g., task difficulty, task complexity, task familiarity) without giving enough attention to the actual role of task in user studies (i.e., whether task was answered or merely served as a context for eliciting relevance judgment). However, the roles of work tasks and search tasks in human-information interaction may affect a series of behavioral and cognitive factors, including user motivations, cognitive effort/task load, search tactics, and the consequences of search activities (Byström and Hansen, 2005; Huvila, 2008; Liu, 2017). For instance, a SIGIR2013 paper (DOI: 10.1145/2484028.2484050) reports on a longitudinal study where researchers asked participants to conduct a work task (i.e., writing project), define their own search tasks, and interact with the experimental interfaces. Under this circumstance, work task may have a much stronger effect on the information-seeking episode compared to the cases where participants were merely asked to find documents relevant to a given task (in fact, one or two paragraphs of search task description).

4.3   SUMMARY

This chapter explains the facets and dimensions of IIR user studies and emphasizes the potential relationships among them. Research focus and problems are the roots of user studies based on which researchers decide specific variables, participants, tasks, system and interface features, as well as behavioral measures and models for data analysis. We illustrate our faceted framework in a representative example of IIR user studies (i.e., Bron et al., 2013). In addition, we also discussed several ignored and under-reported facets and factors that may significantly affect the final results and outputs of the entire user study procedure.

In Chapter 5 we will apply the faceted framework illustrated here in deconstructing, explaining, and evaluating the decisions and compromises made in IIR user study design.

CHAPTER 5

Evaluating IIR User Studies of Different Types

Chapter 4 covered in detail the main facets of IIR user studies and some of the underlying connections among these facets. To support our arguments around the proposed framework, we use the-state-of-the-art user studies selected from multiple IR and HCI venues as examples to illustrate the facets and the associated subfacets that emerged from our paper coding process.

In this chapter, the faceted framework is applied in evaluating IIR user studies of different types. The evaluation of IIR user studies should consider not only the individual facets and components, but also the role and effects of the connections and "collaborations" among different facets. As discussed in previous chapters, the ideal situation of user study design is an effective balance among different facets and components. The effectiveness of a multi-facet balance refers to the extent to which the combination of a series of facet values can properly address the proposed research problem(s).

A study design compromise made in some aspects is usually for the purpose of obtaining benefits from other aspects. For instance, although in-situ or real-time judgment of document usefulness and search satisfaction may be intrusive to the search process (and thereby may affect the realism of search behavior data), it may help guarantee the accuracy of usefulness judgments as participants can make judgments in real-time searching instead of trying to recall their past search experiences from their limited short-term memory in a post-search questionnaire or interview. Thus, despite the limitation, this design decision can be a good choice for a research on the comparison between in-situ and post-search usefulness judgments (meta-evaluation of usefulness judgment metrics). However, the limitation caused by this decision could become a major problem if the research goal is to understand users' web search strategies in local steps (due to the intrusiveness). Therefore, the benefits and limitations of a user study design (i.e., facet values and the potential connections among them) should be evaluated based upon the research questions it seeks to address. In this chapter, we apply the faceted framework in IIR user study evaluation based on the following two premises:

- the strengths and weaknesses of a user study should be evaluated with respect to its ability in answering the proposed research question(s); and

- a user study can be deconstructed as a combination of several interrelated facet values.

According to the first premise, the values of the major facets should be determined according to the specific research focus and problem(s). The second premise suggests that different facets or dimensions cannot be evaluated in a separate, individual manner. Instead, we should focus on how different facet values interact and "collaborate" in facilitate the investigation of research problems. The existing works on IR study evaluation mainly focus on data analysis and the statistical result reporting practice (e.g., Sakai, 2016) or report a small set of user study components separately without fully revealing the possible connections among them (e.g., Kelly and Sugimoto, 2013). To address this issue and to emphasize the role of the connections among different facets of user studies, we employ our faceted framework in evaluating different *combinations of facet values* that represent different decisions and even compromises made in varying problem spaces.

In the following sections, we explain the idea of faceted evaluation in the three types of user studies respectively (i.e., understanding user behavior and experience, IIR system/interface features evaluation, meta-evaluation of evaluation metrics). To fully illustrate the connections among facets and evaluate divergent study design decisions, we apply the faceted framework in evaluating a set of representative user studies reported in recently published research papers. Given the comprehensiveness of our faceted framework, it is safe to say that our approach can be applied in evaluating a wide range of IIR user studies.

5.1   UNDERSTANDING USER BEHAVIOR AND EXPERIENCE

In faceted evaluation, we first selected and focused on a series of major facets based on the research focus and questions, aiming to accurately identify and represent the major decisions and compromises made in study design. Specifically, for each examined user study under the corresponding category (here it is *understanding user behavior and experience*), we reviewed the values of the subfacets (i.e., independent variable, quasi-independent variable, dependent variable) under the facet, *variable*, and assessed the implicit connections between them and the values of other relevant facets and subfacets in our framework. Our core argument behind this approach is that the decision on and evaluation of one facet value should take into consideration other relevant facet values and their impacts on the procedure and results of the study.

For instance, in Edwards and Kelly (2017), researchers used both task and SERP quality to manipulate participants' emotional states in web search in a within-subjects design study. In this case, our major facets and subfacets of interest in evaluation include: search task and topic, system interface elements varied (SERP quality), search behavior and experience. Given the goal of this research (inferring emotion from behavior in search tasks), researchers assigned *evaluate* tasks in the study as these tasks are engaging and complex enough to elicit multi-round, rich interactions between users and systems in laboratory settings. The task topics were varied so that researchers can better control the effects of specific topics and observe relatively "clean" task effects. Liu et al. (2019)

employed similar strategy (designing different topics for the same task types) in order to separate the behavioral impacts caused by topics and tasks.

Beside the values in individual main facets that are directly associated with the predefined research problem, in the faceted evaluation we also considered the facets and subfacets which were directly related to the balance between the major facets. Specifically, in Edwards and Kelly (2017), we found that the method of statistical modeling (i.e., hierarchical linear model) should be taken into account for user study evaluation as it controls the random effects caused by task time, which can be of help in at least partially controlling the potential negative effect of not controlling search task completion time (the researchers did not set a time limit for completing the tasks). Under this circumstance, researchers did a good job in reaching a balance among interrelated facet values: elicit relatively natural search behavior from the task context with no arbitrary time limit (to meet the major research goal) and also control the variation caused by this design choice at the statistical level.

It is worth noting that interventions on system and/or interface components have been used in both search behavior exploration and IIR evaluation research (e.g., Kelly and Azzopardi, 2015; Klouche et al., 2015; Ruotsalo et al., 2018; Shah, Pickens, and Golovchinsky, 2010; Turpin, Kelly, and Arguello, 2016; Umemoto, Yamamoto, and Tanaka, 2016). The major difference is that in search behavior research involving human experience or cognition, system and interface features are usually designed or implemented as tools to manipulate user-side variables at different levels (e.g., behavior, cognition, experience and engagement), whereas in IIR evaluation studies, system and interface features themselves are treated as the research focuses and are evaluated from the user's perspective. Therefore, in user behavior and experience studies, it is critical to evaluate the effectiveness of the system-based human factor manipulation that serve as the cornerstone for other components of user studies. In Edwards and Kelly's (2017) case, the effectiveness of SERP-quality-based manipulation of user frustration was verified by a set of survey-based standard ground truth measures. Hence, the quality of user feature manipulation and search perception measurements as two separate facets are closely related in this case. Similarly, in another example, Ong et al. (2017) used SERPs of varying qualities to manipulate information scent level (as a part of information foraging context) and verified the effectiveness of this manipulation via external assessors' annotations. These designs and reporting practices can facilitate the explanation of researchers' decisions in "facet engineering" and can help readers and reviewers evaluate the validity of the designed interventions and manipulations as well as the reliability of the conclusions drawn from the user study.

As an illustration and application, we employed our faceted framework in evaluating the user study reported in Edwards and Kelly (2017) (see the facet map in Figure 5.1).

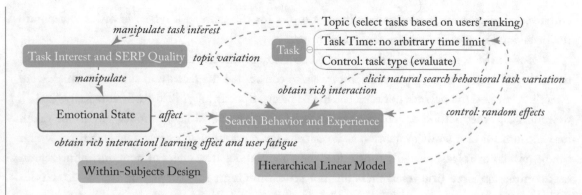

Figure 5.1: Faceted evaluation example: a facet map.

Despite the uniqueness of every specific user study, the faceted framework consisting of generalizable facets and subfacets can still be applied in deconstructing, characterizing, and evaluating a wide spectrum of IIR research. With this unified faceted framework, researchers can better extract, summarize, and manage the metadata of user studies.

In general, when evaluating a user study using the faceted framework, one can start with the core facets (e.g., independent and dependent variables, task features) identified according to the research focus as they should be the top priority for the study. Then, the researchers can gradually expand the evaluation analysis by incorporating other relevant facets (e.g., recruitment, participants' motivations and knowledge background, statistical analysis) which are manipulated to keep the balance among facets, provide additional supports for answering the questions, and compensate for the limitations of the study design compromises made in other dimensions.

During this process, the researcher should consider and evaluate: (1) the quality and usefulness of each individual facet value in the entire study (e.g., the quality of task, the usefulness of system component(s) in manipulating users' perceptions); and (2) the role and structure of the connections among different facet values. For instance, in the case presented in Figure 5.1, we started with the research questions and associated variables (emotional states as independent variables, search behavior and experience as dependent variables) and identified the *core balance* here: making decisions and compromises in some of the task aspects to ensure the successful manipulation of emotional state (which is the top priority and main focus of the user study). On the dependent variable side, a variety of design decisions were also made for the purpose of obtaining rich search interaction data (e.g., within-subjects design, no time limit for search session, restrict task type to evaluate task only). Then, with respect to the multi-facet connections and collaborations, we took into account the techniques and the associated facets involved in controlling the damages or limitations caused by the aforementioned design decisions (e.g., statistical methods, randomize topic order).

Our faceted analysis indicates that the overall design decision made here were well aligned with the proposed research goals, and that several manipulations in other facets (e.g., study procedure design, statistical analysis) can help to partially compensate the limitations from the study design compromises. It is worth noting that no user study design is perfect with no limitation. There are still some potential damages caused by the study design decisions that were not well controlled (e.g., possible effects of topic variations and user fatigue). The mission of our faceted scheme is to facilitate an in-depth reflection and assessment of user study design (especially the compromises made) by deconstructing a study into interrelated facets and dimensions and clarifying the facet values and the roles of the collaborations among them in helping answer the research questions (e.g., manipulating experimental conditions, controlling the context of search interaction, damage control for the study design compromises in other facets).

The faceted scheme offers a unified skeleton of IIR user studies and can be embodied with the tools, methods, and components designed in specific research contexts. The evaluations of facets and facet connections illustrated above could not be conducted without the proposed approach. In a common baseline situation (i.e., evaluating user study without the faceted scheme), there are several limitations that may significantly reduce the validity and usefulness of the evaluation. For instance, the "baseline evaluations" are often incomplete as only a small portion of the facets (e.g., sample size, task type, experimental system) are discussed and many are highly relevant but under-reported facets (e.g., work task scenario, incentives for participation) are ignored. Additionally, almost all of the existing user study evaluations consider different user study dimensions separately, which hinders the examinations of the roles of and the connections among different facets in specific research contexts. After all, in a valid user study, different facets and components should "work together" and jointly support the researcher's pursuit of knowledge.

5.2   SYSTEM/INTERFACE FEATURES EVALUATION

With respect to system or interface evaluation research, researchers usually manipulate one or more system features and evaluate the proposed new feature(s) with users. Despite the divergence among different specific research topics, most of this type of studies are built upon two common fundamental components: system and evaluation.

In terms of the manipulated systems or interface features, to better examine the causality between system changes and variations in search interactions, in previous studies researchers usually chose to control all other aspects of the system and contextual features (e.g., SERP, search collection, task) and clearly define the baseline condition(s). The main reason for this control is that when a system or interface is varied in multiple aspects and largely diverges from baseline systems, it would be difficult to figure out which component or feature plays the major role in affecting the independent variables. As a result of this design decision (manipulate one or a small set of factors and control others), users' search behaviors were usually studied in relatively unrealistic laboratory settings (e.g., interacting with SERPs which only present ten organic results, searching on test collections which only include newspaper documents). For example, in Syed and Collins-Thompson (2017), researchers only employed vocabulary learning tasks, aiming to measure learning effectiveness and evaluate the proposed new algorithm in a relatively "clean" manner. Despite the (unrealistic) restriction on task type, this compromise enabled researchers to quantitatively evaluate human learning and search algorithm performance and thereby allowed them to at least partially address the proposed research problems. Another risk of this type of system features control is that when the system or interface change(s) is too subtle, it may become very difficult to detect any significant variation in user behavior and experience. This risk could become a serious problem in small-scale user studies as the sample size may not be big enough for statistical models to capture any statistically significant difference. (In other words, the analysis is underpowered.) Under this circumstance, given the statistically non-significant results, it would be difficult for researchers to differentiate the sample size issue from the intervention design problem.

In addition, to properly evaluate system features with users, researchers have to choose appropriate baseline system(s) or interface(s) (included in system feature facet) and ground truths (captured by behavior and experience facet) based on their specific research topics and contexts (e.g., task, background of participants, search collections). As discussed before, due to the controls in study design, the proposed new system or interface are usually very similar if not exactly the same to the baseline system except for the manipulated feature. For instance, in the user study presented by Umemoto, Yamamoto, and Tanaka (2016), the only difference between the treatment system and baseline system is the proposed additional feature (i.e., with or without a visualization of potentially missed information).

Differing from simple, one-feature manipulation, there are also some other experimental systems that tended to be a little bit complex and involve multiple new features (e.g., Bateman, Teevan, and White, 2012; Htun, Halvey, and Baillie, 2017). In these studies, the experimental systems or tools can support more complex, innovative search interactions (e.g., sharing query and search result history, making bookmarks and notes, reviewing the metadata about past search interactions) and thereby can elicit richer interaction and feedback data from participants. However, for the researchers conducting these studies, separating the effects from different system features and affordances in data analysis often turn out to be one of the major challenges.

With respect to the collection of ground truth information, the ground truth should also be evaluated according to the specific research questions as well as the quality (i.e., reliability and validity) of the measures involved (e.g., scales and questionnaires, signals associated with specific devices). For example, in Kelly and Azzopardi (2015), researchers intended to evaluate the effects of SERP size based on user behavior and experience, including workload in search. To this end, they added the relevant items extracted from the NASA Task Load Index into a post-search questionnaire to collect workload information. Similarly, when evaluating a system feature based on search satisfaction (e.g., Umemoto, Yamamoto, and Tanaka, 2016), researchers often adopt user annotated search satisfaction as ground truth for user-oriented system evaluation. In addition, to preparing ground truth measure related to document judgments, researchers often invite external assessors to assess the usefulness and relevance of the documents included in test collections (e.g., TREC session track relevance judgment[3]). These ground truth measures serve as basic cornerstones of IIR evaluation and directly contribute to the integration of user characteristics with system evaluation and design.

The selection and evaluation of ground truth information or measure is a critical component of evaluation-oriented IR studies and is often closely related to the nature of users' self-reported data: user-reported satisfaction and experience are usually very subjective in nature and may cause unexpected variations in system evaluation results. Also, some of the existing user experience measures (e.g., satisfaction, difficulty) may consist of multiple divergent or even opposite dimensions (e.g., satisfaction level on search result ranking and presentation, interface design, query reformulation support; difficulty in formulating query, difficulty in evaluating the usefulness of search results). Consequently, the self-reported data may contain a variety of mixed effects and thereby generate misleading results. These problems could become very severe when participants' background vary over multiple dimensions (e.g., language, system familiarity, knowledge background, topic familiarity).

Many practical strategies associated with other facets have been employed in previous studies to at least partially compensate for the potential limitations discussed above. For example, before assigning formal search tasks, a training task or tutorial video was usually presented to users to ensure a similar level of system familiarity at the beginning of formal study procedure (included under the subfacet, *pre-study training*, of the *study procedure* facet (e.g., Bron et al., 2013; Cole et al., 2014; Lagun et al., 2014; Umemoto, Yamamoto, and Tanaka, 2016). The potential effect of language proficiency on task performance and system use can be controlled at the recruitment stage (e.g., Syed and Collins-Thompson, 2017). Note that most of these damage control techniques can also be applied in some other similar research contexts and problem spaces. In addition to these widely applied, procedure-oriented strategies, we also need to dig deeper into the nature of several frequently used ground truth measures, such as relevance, usefulness, and satisfaction. Deconstructing these complex concepts into different dimensions and measuring these dimensions separately could be useful for developing a deeper, more accurate understanding of the ground truth measures (Cole et al., 2009; Saracevic, 1975; Zhang et al., 2014).

In sum, the evaluation of system or interface features evaluation research also follows the procedure explained in the previous section and requires a deep reflection on the implicit connections among different facet values. Specifically, the evaluation should start with the predefined re-

---

[3] https://trec.nist.gov/data/session/2014/README.txt.

search focus and related core facets. Using these facets, one can properly deconstruct the major parts of the user study at hand. In system or interface features evaluation research, the core facets usually include system feature (which can depict system or interface feature manipulation) and behavior and experiences (which include the user experience and performance evaluation metrics). Digging into the connections among these core facets as well as their associations with other relevant facets (e.g., language and education background of participants, pre-study training, or warm up task) can help us understand the strengths and limitations caused by the study decision decisions and the methods employed to compensate for the associated limitations. Therefore, compared to examining different aspects of user studies separately, building a multi-level facet map (from core facets to external relevant facets) based on our faceted framework can better facilitate user study evaluation as it enables researchers to evaluate the design decisions, compromises and compensations within a network of interrelated facets and factors.

5.3   META-EVALUATION OF EVALUATION MEASURES

Similar to system or interface features evaluation, meta-evaluation of evaluation metrics also contains several evaluation-related components or facets and involves ground truth selections. However, in this type of research, the evaluation is conducted by comparing and judging different evaluation measures, rather than IR systems. In the context of IIR studies, meta-evaluation analysis usually involves the comparison between system-oriented performance measures, user-reported measures, and search behavior measures of different types. Given the rapid development of feature extraction and feature engineering techniques, to better capture user characteristics in IR, recent works also take into account other rarely used user-oriented features, such as facial expression and physiological features (e.g., Gwizdka et al., 2017; Gwizdka and Zhang, 2015; Moshfeghi and Jose, 2013). This improvement in feature diversity creates more room for meta-evaluation as well as the development of user behavioral modeling.

As a type of evaluation studies, meta-evaluation of evaluation measures also faces the ground truth problem, which usually involves the subfacets under the behavioral and experience facet. To evaluate the effectiveness of system-oriented (e.g., Mean Average Precision, normalized Discounted Cumulative Gain) and user-centered evaluation measures, researchers compared them with user reported ground truth, such as users' query-level and session-level satisfaction, in-situ and post-search relevance judgments, and experienced work and cognitive loads, aiming to figure out if these features are indicative of at least some aspects of user judgment, experience, and search performance (e.g., Jiang, He, and Allan, 2017; Luo et al., 2017; Smucker and Jethani, 2010). While this approach enables the evaluation of evaluation metrics with users, it also comes with the challenges and limitations discussed above (e.g., individual differences, internal subjectivity and complexity of self-reported measures). Hence, a solid evaluation of ground truth measure(s) is a critical component of the user study evaluation here. Without a reliable ground truth measure, the entire evaluation study would collapse.

In addition to the ground truth problem, there is a paradox in meta-evaluation research, which often requires researchers to make compromises and tough choices in study design: meta-evaluation of evaluation metrics need to be conducted based on a relatively large, session-level dataset which usually includes both search behavior data and annotations from users and/or external assessors. However, in the context of controlled laboratory studies, it is often hard to recruit a large group of participants doing complex search and annotation tasks. Consequently, researchers usually find it difficult to definitively answer an IIR evaluation question with user studies data.

The most common compromise made to resolve this paradox is asking participants to do more search sessions (described by the subfacet called *amount of tasks*), usually in within-subjects design (included in the *experimental design* facet), for ensuring the richness of search and annotation data. For instance, in Luo et al. (2017), each participant conducted 20 tasks within 2 h in a controlled lab environment. Although this data collection strategy can improve the richness of data and help control individual differences, as a compromise it comes with a series of limitations, such as potential learning effect and user fatigue. Fortunately, a variety of compensations can partially mitigate the negative effect of these limitations. For example, when doing complex search and annotation tasks, participants were asked to take a break between tasks to reduce possible fatigue (recorded under *quality control* facet) (e.g., Jiang, He, and Allan, 2017). Also, the learning effects in doing a sequence of search tasks can be mitigated by randomized task order (characterized under the *task* facet) (e.g., Mao et al., 2016).

In sum, for the evaluation of meta-evaluation user studies, one should also start with the specific research focuses (e.g., system-oriented features, search behavior features, physiological and emotional indicators), deconstruct the study design into facets and reorganize them as a facet map consisting of multiple levels of interrelated facets and factors. In faceted evaluation, the core facets directly related to the major goals and study design compromises should be identified (e.g., behavior and experience, task) and analyzed based upon their roles in addressing the proposed research problems. Then, other relevant subfacets can be added around the core facets in the facet map. The facet values as well as the potential connections among them should be identified and evaluated based on the extent to which the design decisions and manipulations in these subfacets jointly help answer the research questions and/or control the "damages" caused by the aforementioned study design decisions.

5.4   SUMMARY

This chapter explained and illustrated the faceted evaluation approach in three different lines of user studies. Particularly, we proposed a multi-faceted, replicable evaluation method, *facet mapping*, in order to facilitate the deconstruction of complex user study design and also to support the construction of facet networks in analyzing the connections and "collaborations" among different facets (see Figure 5.1). Given the goals of faceted user study evaluation, the main missions of facet map are: (1) identify the main facets and components of a user study; and (2) clarify the roles of different facet values as well as the underlying connections among them in answering the predefined research questions (e.g., manipulating experimental conditions, controlling the context of search interaction, damage control for the study design compromises in other facets). The faceted evaluation should include both the assessment of each individual facet (e.g., the quality of task description and experimental system) and (more importantly) the evaluation of the collaboration among different facets within the same research context.

Improving the characterization and evaluation of IIR user studies will create sizable impacts on multiple aspects of IIR research and also lead to new challenges and opportunities for future works. Based upon the previously explained structure and missions of the faceted scheme, the following chapters will further discuss the implications of this faceted framework for IIR user study design, reporting and evaluation practices as well as the possible directions for future works in related areas.

CHAPTER 6

Implications and Limitations of the Faceted Framework

As reported in previous chapters, we conducted an in-depth systematic review of 462 IIR user study papers recently published in several top IR venues, including SIGIR, CHIIR, CHI, *JASIST*, *IP&M*, and *ACM TOIS*. Based on the coding analysis of the collected papers, we developed a faceted framework consisting of multiple interrelated facets and explained how this faceted approach can be applied as a standard approach to deconstruct, characterize IIR user studies (i.e., identify the related facets and build a facet map), and thereby to evaluate the strengths and weakness of various study design decisions with respect to answering the proposed research questions (i.e., examine how the manipulations in multiple facets help or fail to address the research problems and/or control the "damage" of compromises). Hence, we believe that the faceted framework presented here has the potential to help students and young researchers in the area of IIR to design and assess their own studies.

Despite the strengths of the faceted framework discussed in previous chapters, it still has limitations and faces unresolved issues in several aspects. We believe that these limitations and challenges can generate new opportunities for future researchers to further improve IIR study design, reporting, and evaluation practices. The implications and limitations of our work are discussed in detail in the following sections.

6.1 IMPLICATIONS FOR INTERACTION IR USER STUDY DESIGN AND EVALUATION

The faceted framework construes user studies as combinations of multiple levels of facets values. This approach has several practical implications for future IIR user studies, including on the structure and reporting practice of a user study, the design and manipulation of its facets, and how various facets are combined in different ways. We will shed some light on these implications.

The structure of a user study: The faceted evaluation framework does not merely consider one or two factors or dimensions. Instead, it encourages IIR researchers to look at the whole structure of user studies and to fully understand the connections and collaborations among them in specific research contexts. When designing or evaluating an IIR user research, one can start with identifying the core facets and major study design decisions that are directly related to the research questions. Then, the user study can incorporate more relevant facets that can help answer the research question(s) and/or control the negative effects of the major compromises. Through mapping the strengths and limitations of design decisions and compromises to the related facets and building a facet map, we can better reflect on the connections between different dimensions of user study in context and evaluate the strengths and weakness of user study design.

The design and manipulation of facets: As it is illustrated in Chapter 4, the essence of a user study is a unique combination of multiple, interrelated facet values. When making choices in determining facet values (i.e., deciding task type, designing system feature), one should ask and answer the following questions.

1. Can these manipulations and designs help answer the research questions?

2. What are the implicit compromises and limitations behind these manipulations on study design?

3. Is there any way to mitigate the negative effects of these compromises?

By answering these questions, one can better explore and evaluate the interactions among different facets within a specific research context (e.g., a manipulation in one facet can compensate for the limitations caused by the design choice in another facet).

Understanding the connections and interactions among the facets of user study can help IIR researchers design and manipulate (if necessary) user study components in such ways that different facets and components can "collaborate" with each other (e.g., "working together" in controlling contextual factors; creating different contexts and environments of search; mitigating the negative effects of the study design compromises made in other dimensions) in addressing the research problems of interest.

Innovative combinations of facets: Examining and evaluating innovative combinations of facets may break new ground for IIR research. For instance, applying neuro-physiological features (see Gwizdka and Mostafa, 2017) in a field context may enhance our understanding of how people distribute their attention resources and run their mental models when searching for information and interacting with search systems in the wild. Designing and comparing different combinations of work task and search task (e.g., learning tasks in workplaces versus learning tasks in school environments) can also help us better explore users' task-based information search behavior as well as the interactions between different levels of task contexts (Byström and Hansen, 2005). Besides, new combinations of facets and factors can be used to test innovative theories and models of search interactions, such as click models of different types (e.g., Borisov et al., 2018; Li et al., 2014) and economic models of information seeking and search (e.g., Azzopardi, 2014; Liu, 2017, 2019).

In summary, testing new facet values and exploring innovative combinations of facets can help researchers create new user study vectors consisting of multiple facet values, and thereby may expand the research problem space in which the user study approach as an enriched, useful methodology can be applied and evaluated in meaningful ways.

6.2   IMPLICATIONS FOR IIR USER STUDY REPORTING PRACTICES

In addition to the aforementioned implications for study design and evaluation, the idea of examining, connecting, and organizing facets can also offer insights for IIR user study reporting practices.

Report the design choices in different facets and their roles: Reporting practice is the basis of user study evaluation. Our faceted evaluation framework was constructed based upon a series of state-of-the-art IIR user studies reported in the research papers recently published in several top venues. Also, to perform a comprehensive faceted evaluation, researchers need to obtain enough details regarding user study design from published research papers and reports. Poor reporting practices in published papers can cause huge issues for meta-evaluations (Kelly and Sugimoto, 2013; O'Brien and McCay-Peet, 2017; Sakai, 2016), not to mention the difficulty in interpreting the study results and implications. To clarify the structure of a user study and the roles of different components as well as the connections among them, researchers need to consider and discuss the three aforementioned questions associated with the design and manipulation in facets. By doing so, future researchers can better understand the rationales of the specific design choices and evaluate these choices based on the specific research questions and problem spaces.

Report the commonly under-reported facets and factors. The under-reported facets and factors identified in the previous sections need to be reported in user study papers (especially when these facets are directly related to the research questions and study design compromises) as they may offer important cues for interpreting the variations in results. For example, when the research goal is measuring participants' knowledge gain and search performance in a controlled experimental setting, it is critical to also examine the possible effects of language (e.g., participants' native language, language used in presenting study materials), topic-independent search skills, and participants' motivations to participate (e.g., the structure of incentives). With respect to the task facet, to fully understand the effects of search task facets (e.g., task goal, task product, task stage, task complexity and prior determinability), researchers need to first investigate the overarching work tasks or problematic situations and their associations with the search tasks defined in the user study (Belkin, 2008). Examining and reporting the critical under-reported facets can help expand the research in IR to take a broader perspective of the information seeking and search processes and to include more user characteristics and contextual features. As a result, we may be able to obtain a deeper, more comprehensive understanding on the dynamic associations between user characteristics, behavioral patterns, and contextual factors identified in the past user studies (e.g., Jiang, He, and Allan, 2017; Liu et al., 2010, 2019).

6.3   LIMITATIONS AND CHALLENGES

This work sought to develop a multi-faceted evaluation framework based on state-of-the-art IIR user studies and to fully explore the richness of user study facets and the relations among them via a faceted approach. Beside the implications discussed above, there are also two main limitations related to our analysis: the sources of our data, and the method we have applied for analyzing/ coding it.

Source of data: We conducted our analysis based on a narrowly defined set of IIR user study papers, and it is important to be mindful of this when drawing conclusions. However, since the six venues from which we extracted user study papers are major scholarly communication venues for the IR community and usually publish high-quality, state-of-the-art IIR papers, selecting papers and developing a coding scheme from this paper pool can to some extent guarantee the quality and generalizability of the proposed faceted framework in future evaluation. Nevertheless, it is still possible that we missed out some subfacets, factors, or specific techniques discussed and/or manipulated in the research papers published in some other IR-related venues (e.g., WWW, WSDM, CIKM, ICTIR, JCDL, and ASIS&T AM).

Reliability of coding: Many of the facet values in the published research papers are not very straightforward (e.g., task type, source of tasks, user characteristics), which makes it difficult to extract these facets in some cases. Besides, the coding analysis in our work was qualitative in nature for most of the facets and thus not as replicable as the analysis of statistical measures (e.g., Sakai, 2016). A broader scope of coding analysis may help validate the existing faceted evaluation framework and revise some parts of it when necessary.

In addition to the limitations discussed above, IIR user studies also face several challenges based on which several additional implications could be proposed for the IR community.

Reporting practice: The under-reported facets and missed information concerning research context (e.g., task source, time length of the study) often lead to gaps and blind spots in the facet network of user studies. These blind spots may eventually prevent researchers from conducting a more comprehensive, in-depth meta-evaluation of user study and make it difficult to explain some of the patterns extracted from data (Kelly and Sugimoto, 2013). Also, the relationships between different aspects and dimensions (e.g., participants and tasks, experimental search system features and behavioral measures) in user study design are not always clear in the reported IIR user studies. Future IIR research should improve their reporting practices and clarify the connections between the main facets (including commonly under-reported facets), research questions and focuses, and the compromises made in study design. Additionally, in evaluation-oriented studies, researchers also need to clearly explain the rationale of adopting a particular ground truth measure(s) and report the process of evaluating ground truth measure(s). The proposed faceted framework can serve as a toolkit for study design and a checklist for IIR user study reporting practices.

Replication study: Despite the similarities in multiple facets, user studies are usually uniquely designed for their respective research questions that may involve largely different systems, tasks, and user populations. As a result, each IIR user study appears to be an isolated island and thus cannot be quantitatively and collectively evaluated. To resolve this issue, major IR venues (e.g., SIGIR, CLEF) encourage researchers to replicate existing user studies and test the reliability and validity of the associated results (Ferro et al., 2016; Ferro and Kelly, 2018; Suominen et al., 2018). However, future research efforts and new platforms are still needed for replication studies in both field and controlled lab settings to answer two empirical questions: (1) Are the conclusions drawn from previous user studies reliable? (2) Would a change in user study facet(s) (especially the under-reported facets) significantly alter the results of a user study?

To address the meta-issues of replicating user studies, HCI researchers organized the RepliCHI workshop in the SIGCHI community to discuss the significant findings and contributions from revisiting works (cf. Wilson et al., 2014). However, the idea and movement of RepliCHI was ultimately rejected by the community as it was considered be to only relevant to a small sub-community of HCI research. In contrast, given the longstanding emphasis on evaluation in IR, developing new framework and methods to facilitate replication studies would certainly be of interest to the entire community. Opening a new track for user study replication and addressing the two aforementioned questions can help the IR community better answer the research questions of interest and properly evaluate the existing user study facets as well as the entire toolkit.

"Bad" results presentation: In most, if not all, of the published IR empirical studies, researchers successfully obtained "right" results that confirm at least some of the research hypotheses, theories, and arguments. However, it is worth noting that in a wide range of unpublished user studies, researchers actually encountered unexpected, "bad" results which fail to respond to the research questions in expected way(s): For instance, in some user studies, none of the proposed research hypotheses are confirmed by the collected empirical evidences; the prediction performance of new model is significantly worse than that of the baselines; most of the statistical test results (e.g., coefficients of regression models, differences between predefined groups) are not statistically significant, and so on. These surprises and "bad" results often get unnoticed and are kept unpublished. Yet, if we carefully examine the facets of the user studies behind these "bad" results, they may become important gateways towards striking findings and/or methodological innovations.

Aside from the surprising findings that result in quantum leaps and unexpected innovations in the corresponding research areas, we also need to explore other possible reasons (especially unnoticed problems) that create unexpected, "bad" results in data analyses. The existence of unexpected results may ultimately lead our attention to a series of critical, under-reported facets and factors. With respect to the participants and systems, for example, participants may come from largely different knowledge background and thus have a very different understanding of the same task descriptions.

Also, in some IIR evaluation studies, the variation in system affordances may be too subtle. Consequently, users' search behavioral signals are not sensitive enough to capture the implicit variations. In crowdsourcing user studies, the lack of data quality control methods may lead to biased and contaminated results in analyses. Besides, the adoption of specific search behavior and experience measures can also determine the significance and direction of the results. Specifically, for instance, compared to browsing and search result examination behaviors, the users' query formulation strategies may be more sensitive to external treatments and interventions. Similarly, compared to the task-level measures, task-stage or action-level dual-task measures can better capture the variations in users' perceived levels of cognitive loads (Gwizdka, 2010). Establishing a new platform (e.g., forum, workshop on bad results and possibly problematic designs of user studies) for researchers to present, re-analyze, and openly discuss "bad" results can largely enhance our understanding of the roles of different facets as well as the possible ways in which an IIR user study design can go wrong.

The bridges between small-scale user studies and large-scale IR experiments: It is certainly useful to learn about user characteristics and search interaction patterns in small-scale, laboratory studies with well-controlled conditions. However, it is also important to explore the possible connections and implicit bridges between small-scale user studies and large-scale IR experiments. The application and generalization of the findings from small-scale user studies can be highly valuable for search systems design and evaluation. To fully understand these implicit connections, we need to at least answer the following questions.

1. To what extent can we generalize the models we learned from small-scale user studies to large-scale datasets collected in the wild (e.g., large-scale search log data collected through commercial search engines, data from TREC, CLEF, and NTCIR)?

2. To what extent can we automatically extract the main facet values directly from large-scale search log data (e.g., task facets, session lengths, search behavioral measures) and use them in experiments in various ways (e.g., as features in predictive models; as ground truth for evaluation; as feedbacks or rewards for reinforcement learning)?

3. Based on the findings from small-scale user studies, what assumptions can we make about different user study facets in order to support large-scale IR experiments where high-quality, complete user annotation data is not always available?

Answering these questions can help us better clarify the contributions of and the connections between small-scale IIR user studies and large-scale IR experiments.

CHAPTER 7

Conclusion and Future Directions

According to the cognitive viewpoint of IR research, search systems are essentially interactive and hence users should not be abstracted out of system design and evaluation processes (Belkin, 2015; Ingwersen, 1996). To understand the role of users in search interaction and to evaluate IR systems with users, IIR researchers often design user studies of different types to examine various elements, dimensions, and stages of the information search and evaluation process. Therefore, to sharpen the instruments of IIR user studies and to improve the reliability and validity of the associated conclusions, it is critical to develop a comprehensive, generalizable framework for characterizing, reporting, evaluating IIR user studies.

To this end, we developed a faceted framework for user study evaluation based on a systematic review and coding analysis of 462 state-of-the-art IIR research papers recently published in several top venues, including ACM SIGIR conferences (2000-2018), CHIIR conferences (2016-2018), *Journal of the Association for Information Science and Technology* (*JASIST*), *Information Processing and Management* (*IP&M*), CIII conferences, and *ACM Transactions on Information Systems* (*ACM TOIS*). Our paper reviewing and coding procedure was introduced in Chapter 3. Built upon the systematic user study review, In Chapters 4 and 5, we illustrated the main facets and factors of the framework with specific user study examples and also explained in detail how our framework can shed lights on the evaluation of IIR user studies of different types. The proposed faceted framework can offer a relatively comprehensive picture of the facets of state-of-the-art IIR user studies and help researchers understand the underlying connections among different facets when evaluating the decisions and compromises made in user study design.

Compared to the existing works on the summarization and evaluation of IR user studies (e.g., Kelly, 2009; Sakai, 2016), our work includes new facets and factors extracted from recently published IR literature and highlights the importance of understanding the connections and "collaborations" between different facets and factors (especially the factors under different facet categories) for characterizing and evaluating IIR user studies. In addition, we use several representative user studies as examples and illustrate how the components and connections embedded in a user study can be deconstructed and analyzed in the light of divergent research questions and contexts.

Despite the strengths and implications of the faceted evaluation framework discussed in the previous chapters, it still has limitations in several aspects (e.g., the scope of paper reviewing in our work, the qualitative nature of paper coding, current reporting practice in IIR community). The limitations are explained in detail in Chapter 6. We believe that these limitations can potentially create new opportunities for researchers in the IR community to further improve IIR study design, reporting, and evaluation practices.

With respect to future directions, there are several ways to improve our faceted scheme and to further enhance our understanding of the roles and potential of IIR user studies. For instance, future research can expand the scope of user study review and include more relevant venues for paper collection and facet extraction, such as ASIS&T, CIKM, JCDL, and so on. By doing so, researchers may be able to identify new subfacets and factors (e.g., new system and/or interface features and search assistant tools, new data collection techniques and associated features, new models for data analysis) and thereby can improve the current version of faceted evaluation framework.

Besides, it is also important to develop new scales, measures, and indicators to quantify the faceted evaluation framework and to improve the generalizability of the framework in evaluating a wide range of IIR user studies. This quantification should include both the measurements of different facets and dimensions (e.g., how many widely-ignored, under-reported subfacets are discussed, which critical statistics are reported) and the quantification of baselines (e.g., a series of interrelated, quantified user study facet measures) for user study evaluation. Due to the fundamental differences among different research focuses and problems, researchers should employ different baselines when evaluating different types of IIR user studies. In addition, as it was discussed in Chapter 6, establishing new platforms (e.g., paper submission tracks, workshops) for reporting replication studies and unexpected results can also deepen our understanding of the potential effects of different facets and dimensions (e.g., task facets, participant or user characteristics, system or interface features) on the results of user studies.

As Robertson (2008) points out, "a field advances not by deciding on a single best compromise, but through different researchers taking different decisions, and the resulting dialectic" (p. 447). In the past two decades, we have witnessed the diversity in user study design manipulations and decisions (e.g., participant recruitment, task design, study device, study procedure, type of data collected) which has largely supported the explorations of users' interactions with search systems in context and significantly expanded the territory of IIR research. By carefully examining and evaluating IIR user studies via the faceted approach, our hope is that the work presented here could add more knowledge about the structure and the related impacts of the "decision in compromise" and better facilitate the dialectic around IIR user study design, reporting, and evaluation.

Appendix

User study annotation example A1: Moshfeghi, Triantafillou, and Pollick (2016)

Research Focus and Variables

[**Research Focus**] understanding search behavior and user cognition [**Keywords** (directly extracted from the paper)] anomalous state of knowledge, information need, information retrieval, fMRI study; [**Independent Variable**] level of information need (IN and no-IN); different scenarios: QA scenario and QAS scenario; [**Dependent Variable**] blood oxygenation level dependent (BOLD) activity in human brain;

Participant

[**Recruitment**] participants were recruited from the participant database at Centre for Cognitive Neuroimaging, University of Glasgow. [**Controlled lab**] Yes; [**Field/Large-scale**] N.A.; [**Sample Size**] 24 participants [**Gender Composition**] 11 males, 13 females; [**Participant Occupation**] no information; [**Age**] all under 44; 18-23 (54.1%) and 30-35 (20.8%); [**Education Background/Level**] no information; [**Participants' Native Language(s)**] 79.1% native English speaker. 20.9% had an advanced level of English; [**Language Used in Study**] English; [**Regular Incentives**] 6 pounds per hour. [**Extra Incentives/Bonus**] no information; [**Length of Study**] about 1 h (50 min to perform all tasks, 10 min to obtain a scan of anatomical structure.

Task

[**Task Source**] experimenter assigned: TREC-8 and TREC 2001 QA tracks- main task; [**Search Task Type**] QA tasks (40 hard and 40 easy); [**Search Task Topic**] topics from TREC QA tracks; [**Number of Tasks**] 80 tasks; [**Number of tasks/Person**] 80 tasks; [**Time Length/Task**] 8 s for question and options presentation, 4-6 s; for transition, no time limit for choosing option; [**Work Task Type**] N.A.; [**Did Work Task**] N.A.; [**Answer Search Task**] choosing option; [**Evaluation Task**] N.A.

Study Procedure and Experimental Design

[**Task/Session Feature Controlled**] two assessors separately judged the difficulty of the questions from TREC QA tracks, and then selected of a subset of questions (40 easy and 40 hard) both annotator agreed upon the difficulty level; [**Task Rotation**] tasks and options within each scenario were randomized; [**Pilot Study**] a pilot study was performed using two participants to confirm that the process worked correctly and smoothly; [**Pre-study Training**] no information; [**Actual Task Completion Time**] no information; [**Quality Control/Data Filtering Criteria**] no information; [**Experimental Design**] within-subjects design.

System Features

[**Study Interface Element Varied**] N.A.; [**Other System/Context Feature Varied**] N.A.; [**Study Apparatus**] image presented using presentation software; fMRI data was collected using a 3T Tim Trio Siemens scanner and 32-channel head coil; [**Search Collection/Corpus**] TREC-8 and TREC-2001 QA tracks main task; [**Ranking Algorithm**] N.A.; [**Non-traditional IR System Assistance Tool**] N.A.

Behavioral and Search Experience Measures

[**Search Behavior Measures**] response to the options; query formulation and document examination in the Scenario 2; [**Instrument for Collecting Search Behavioral Data**] choosing options by pressing buttons; submitting query verbally via a noise-cancelling microphone; [**Relevance Judgment**] N.A.; [**Instrument for Collecting User Judgment**] N.A.; [**Search and System Performance Measures**] N.A.; [**Neuro-physiological Measures**] BOLD activities; [**Instruments for Capturing Neuro-physiological Measures**] image presented using presentation software; fMRI data was collected using a 3T Tim Trio Siemens scanner and 32-channel head coil; [**Offline Information Seeking Behavior**] N.A.; [**Other Information Behavior**] N.A.; [**Data Analysis Method**] multiple linear gression (GLM) for first-level analysis; random effects analysis of variance for second-level analysis; [**Qualitative Analysis**] N.A.; [**Level of Analysis**] task level; [**Task-independent Measures**] no information; [**Task/Session Perception Measures**] post-search questionnaire: the tasks we asked you to perform is (easy/stressful/familiar/clear/satisfactory) answer 1-5 (level of agree); [**Search Experience and System Evaluation Measures**] no information.

Data Analysis and Results

[**Statistical Test Assumption Check Reported**] No; [**Results**] 1. Difference in brain activity due to whether participants experienced IN or not. 2. These differences appeared sensitive to whether or not the IN was associated with actually making a search (or simply deciding that a search would be necessary). 3. A particular region of the brain, posterior cingulate, could be an essential component of IN; [**Effect Size**] reported.

User study annotation example A2: Jiang, He, and Allan (2017).

Research Focus and Variables

[**Research Focus**] meta-evaluation of relevance evaluation metrics; [**Keywords** (directly extracted from the paper)] relevance judgment, search experience, implicit feedback; [**Independent Variable**] in-situ relevance and usefulness judgment, multiple dimensions of judgment; [**Dependent Variable**] post-search relevance/usefulness judgments, post-search search experiences;

Participant

[**Recruitment**] recruited through fliers posted on the campuses of two universities in the U.S. [**Controlled lab**] Yes; [**Field/Large-scale**] N.A.; [**Sample Size**] 28 participants [**Gender Composition**] 12 male, 16 female; [**Participant Occupation**] students; [**Age**] no information; [**Education Background/Level**] undergraduate and graduate; [**Participants' Native Language(s)**] English; [**Language Used in Study**] English; [**Regular Incentives**] $15 per hour; [**Extra Incentives/Bonus**] no information; [**Length of Study**] about 100 min.

Task

[**Task Source**] TREC session tracks; [**Search Task Type**] 4 types (product + goal): factual specific, factual amorphous; intellectual specific, intellectual amorphous.; [**Search Task Topic**] 7 topics; [**Number of Tasks**] 28 tasks; [**Number of tasks/Person**] 4 tasks; [**Time Length/Task**] 10 min per task; [**Work Task Type**] problematic situation/context provided in TREC task descriptions; [**Did Work Task**] N.A.; [**Answer Search Task**] No information; [**Evaluation Task**] post-search judgment stage: rate search experience and finish post-session judgments on each result they visited in the session.

Study Procedure and Experimental Design

[**Task/Session Feature Controlled**] same 4 types for every individual users; [**Task Rotation**] Latin-square rotation; [**Pilot Study**] no information; [**Pre-study Training**] before 4 formal tasks, each participant worked on a training task (including all the steps) for 10 min; [**Actual Task Completion Time**] about 20 min per task; [**Quality Control/Data Filtering Criteria**] only recruited native English speakers to exlude the effect on English fluency on relevance/usefulness judgments; 9 cases of revisitng URL (about 1% of the data) were excluded; the researchers required the participants to take a 5-min break after 2 formal tasks to reduce fatigue; require participants to spend at least 30 s on judging each result in post-search session; [**Experimental Design**] within-subjects design.

System Features

[**Study Interface Element Varied**] N.A.; [**Other System/Context Feature Varied**] N.A.; [**Study Apparatus**] desktop computer; [**Search Collection/Corpus**] open web: filtered Google search results (only include 10-blue links); [**Ranking Algorithm**] N.A.; [**Non-traditional IR System Assistance Tool**] N.A.

Behavioral and Search Experience Measures

[**Search Behavior Measures**] click dwell time; follow-up query features after a target click (URL/title/body); follow-up click features; prior-to-click features (baseline) [information available before users clicking on the result]; [**Instrument for Collecting Search Behavioral Data**] logged by an experimental system; [**Relevance Judgment**] in situ relevance judgment; post-search relevance judgment (TREC web track style: focusing on topical relevance); [**Instrument for Collecting User Judgment**] in situ relevance judgment: recorded by pop-up pages and results logged by experimental system; post-search judgment: post-search survey in judgment stage; [**Search and System Performance Measures**] N.A.; [**Neuro-physiological Measures**] N.A.; [**Instruments for Capturing Neuro-physiological Measures**] N.A.; [**Offline Information Seeking Behavior**] N.A.; [**Other Information Behavior**] N.A.; [**Data Analysis Method**] Pearson's r, Spearman's r, multilevel regression analysis, Prediction: gradient boosted regression trees (GBRT); [**Qualitative Analysis**] N.A.; [**Level of Analysis**] task level; page and action level (e.g., prior-click and post-click actions); [**Task-independent Measures**] pre-search survey: gender, age, degree, search experiences (used in multilevel regression); [**Task/Session Perception Measures**] pre-search survey: task topic familiarity; post-search survey: task difficulty; [**Search Experience and System Evaluation Measures**] post-search survey: satisfaction, frustration, success, total effort, helpness of the system.

Data Analysis and Results

[**Statistical Test Assumption Check Reported**] multi-colinearity checked and reported by using variance inflation factor (VIF); [**Results**] 1 in situ judgments do not exhibit clear benefits over the judgments collected without context (post-session judgment); combing relevance or usefulness with the four alternative judgments (four aspects) improves the correlation with user experience measures; click dwell time is able to predict some but not all dimensions of judgments; current implicit feedback methods plus post-click user interaction can achieve better prediction for all six dimensions of judgments; [**Effect Size**] no information.

Bibliography

Ahn, J. W., Brusilovsky, P., He, D., Grady, J., and Li, Q. (2008). Personalized web exploration with task models. In *Proceedings of the 17th International Conference on World Wide Web* (pp. 1–10). ACM. DOI: 10.1145/1367497.1367499. 7

Aula, A., Khan, R. M., and Guan, Z. (2010). How does search behavior change as search becomes more difficult? In *Proceedings of the SIGCHI Conference on Human Factors in Computing Systems* (pp. 35–44). ACM. DOI: 10.1145/1753326.1753333. 11, 27

Azzopardi, L. (2014). Modelling interaction with economic models of search. In *Proceedings of the 37th International ACM SIGIR Conference on Research and Development in Information Retrieval* (pp. 3–12). ACM. DOI: 10.1145/2600428.2609574. 52

Azzopardi, L., Kelly, D., and Brennan, K. (2013). How query cost affects search behavior. In *Proceedings of the 36th International ACM SIGIR Conference on Research and Development in Information Retrieval* (pp. 23–32). ACM. DOI: 10.1145/2484028.2484049. 7

Bateman, S., Teevan, J., and White, R. W. (2012). The search dashboard: How reflection and comparison impact search behavior. In *Proceedings of the SIGCHI Conference on Human Factors in Computing Systems* (pp. 1785–1794). ACM. DOI: 10.1145/2207676.2208311. 31, 46

Belkin, N. J. (1990). The cognitive viewpoint in information science. *Journal of Information Science*, 16(1), 11-15. DOI: 10.1177/016555159001600104. 1, 2

Belkin, N. J. (2000). Helping people find what they don't know. *Communications of the ACM*, 43(8), 58-61. DOI: 10.1145/345124.345143. 13

Belkin, N. J. (2008). Some (what) grand challenges for information retrieval. In *ACM SIGIR Forum*, 42(1), 47–54. ACM. DOI: 10.1145/1394251.1394261. 15, 53

Belkin, N. J. (2015). Salton award lecture: people, interacting with information. In *Proceedings of the 38th International ACM SIGIR Conference on Research and Development in Information Retrieval* (pp. 1–2). ACM. DOI: 10.1145/2766462.2767854. 16 , 57

Belkin, N., Dumais, S., Scholtz, J., and Wilkinson, R. (2004). Evaluating interactive information retrieval systems: Opportunities and challenges. In *CHI'04 Extended Abstracts on Human Factors in Computing Systems* (pp. 1594–1595). ACM. DOI: 10.1145/985921.986162. 13

Borisov, A., Kiseleva, J., Markov, I., and de Rijke, M. (2018). Calibration: A simple way to improve click models. In *Proceedings of the 27th ACM International Conference on Information and Knowledge Management* (pp. 1503–1506). ACM. DOI: 10.1145/3269206.3269260. 52

Borlund, P. (2016). A study of the use of simulated work task situations in interactive information retrieval evaluations: A meta-evaluation. *Journal of Documentation*, 72(3), 394–413. DOI: 10.1108/JD-06-2015-0068. 30

Bron, M., Van Gorp, J., Nack, F., Baltussen, L. B., and de Rijke, M. (2013). Aggregated search interface preferences in multi-session search tasks. In *Proceedings of the 36th International ACM SIGIR Conference on Research and Development in Information Retrieval* (pp. 123–132). ACM. DOI: 10.1145/2484028.2484050. 35, 40, 47

Büschel, W., Mitschick, A., and Dachselt, R. (2018). Here and now: Reality-based information retrieval: Perspective paper. In *Proceedings of the 2018 Conference on Human Information Interaction and Retrieval* (pp. 171–180). ACM. DOI: 10.1145/3176349.3176384. 8

Byström, K. and Hansen, P. (2005). Conceptual framework for tasks in information studies. *Journal of the American Society for Information science and Technology*, 56(10), 1050–1061. DOI: 10.1002/asi.20197. 30, 39, 52

Capra, R., Arguello, J., Crescenzi, A., and Vardell, E. (2015). Differences in the use of search assistance for tasks of varying complexity. In *Proceedings of the 38th International ACM SIGIR Conference on Research and Development in Information Retrieval* (pp. 23–32). ACM. DOI: 10.1145/2766462.2767741. 21

Capra, R., Arguello, J., O'Brien, H., Li, Y., and Choi, B. (2018). The effects of manipulating task determinability on search behaviors and outcomes. In the *41st International ACM SIGIR Conference on Research and Development in Information Retrieval* (pp. 445–454). ACM. DOI: 10.1145/3209978.3210047. 30

Charmaz, K. (2014). *Constructing Grounded Theory.* Sage Publications: Newbury Park, CA. 21

Chen, Y., Zhou, K., Liu, Y., Zhang, M., and Ma, S. (2017). Meta-evaluation of online and offline Web search evaluation metrics. In *Proceedings of the 39th International ACM SIGIR Conference on Research and Development in Information Retrieval* (pp. 463–472). ACM. DOI: 10.1145/3077136.3080804. 13, 26, 34

Cole, M. J., Gwizdka, J., Liu, C., Belkin, N. J., and Zhang, X. (2013). Inferring user knowledge level from eye movement patterns. *Information Processing and Management*, 49(5), 1075–1091. DOI: 10.1145/2637002.2637011. 2, 28, 34

Cole, M. J., Hendahewa, C., Belkin, N. J., and Shah, C. (2015). User activity patterns during information search. ACM Transactions on Information Systems (TOIS), 33(1), 1. DOI: 10.1145/2699656. 20. 20

Cole, M. J., Hendahewa, C., Belkin, N. J., and Shah, C. (2014). Discrimination between tasks with user activity patterns during information search. In *Proceedings of the 37th International ACM SIGIR Conference on Research and Development in Information Retrieval* (pp. 567–576). ACM. DOI: 10.1145/2600428.2609591. 7, 47

Cole, M., Liu, J., Belkin, N., Bierig, R., Gwizdka, J., Liu, C., Zhang, J. and Zhang, X. (2009). Usefulness as the criterion for evaluation of interactive information retrieval. In *Proceedings of the Third Workshop on Human-Computer Interaction and Information Retrieval (HCIR)*, 1–4. DOI: 10.1.1.221.1557&rep=rep1&type=pdf#page=7. 47

Cooper, H. M. (1989). *Integrating Research: A Guide for Literature Reviews*. Sage Publications: Newbury Park, CA. 15

Deveaud, R., Mothe, J., Ullah, M. Z., and Nie, J. Y. (2018). Learning to adaptively rank document retrieval system configurations. *ACM Transactions on Information Systems (TOIS)*, 37(1), 3. DOI: 10.1145/3231937. 3

Dumais, S., Cutrell, E., Cadiz, J. J., Jancke, G., Sarin, R., and Robbins, D. C. (2016). Stuff I've seen: A system for personal information retrieval and re-use. In *ACM SIGIR Forum*, 49(2), pp. 28–35). ACM. DOI: 10.1145/2888422.2888425. 12

Edwards, A. and Kelly, D. (2017). Engaged or frustrated? Disambiguating emotional state in search. In *Proceedings of the 40th International ACM SIGIR Conference on Research and Development in Information Retrieval* (pp. 125–134). ACM. DOI: 10.1145/3077136.3080818. 8, 10, 18, 34, 42, 43

Eickhoff, C., Dungs, S., and Tran, V. (2015). An eye-tracking study of query reformulation. In *Proceedings of the 38th International ACM SIGIR Conference on Research and Development in Information Retrieval* (pp. 13–22). ACM. DOI: 10.1145/2766462.2767703. 34

Eugster, M. J., Ruotsalo, T., Spapé, M. M., Kosunen, I., Barral, O., Ravaja, N., Jacucci, G. and Kaski, S. (2014). Predicting term-relevance from brain signals. In *Proceedings of the 37th International ACM SIGIR Conference on Research and Development in Information Retrieval* (pp. 425–434). ACM. DOI: 10.1145/2600428.2609594. 34

Feild, H. and Allan, J. (2013). Task-aware query recommendation. In *Proceedings of the 36th International ACM SIGIR Conference on Research and Development in Information Retrieval* (pp. 83–92). ACM. DOI: 10.1145/2484028.2484069. 3

Ferro, N., Fuhr, N., Järvelin, K., Kando, N., Lippold, M., and Zobel, J. (2016). Increasing repro-ducibility in IR: findings from the Dagstuhl Seminar on reproducibility of data-ori-ented experiments in e-science. In *ACM SIGIR Forum*, 50(1), pp. 68–82). ACM. DOI: 10.1145/2964797.2964808. 55

Ferro, N. and Kelly, D. (2018). SIGIR initiative to implement ACM artifact review and badging. In *ACM SIGIR Forum*, 52(1), pp. 4–10). ACM. DOI: 10.1145/3274784.3274786. 55

Gwizdka, J. (2010). Distribution of cognitive load in web search. *Journal of the American Society for Information Science and Technology*, 61(11), 2167–2187. DOI: 10.1002/asi.21385. 11, 56

Gwizdka, J., Hosseini, R., Cole, M., and Wang, S. (2017). Temporal dynamics of eye-tracking and EEG during reading and relevance decisions. *Journal of the Association for Information Science and Technology*, 68(10), 2299–2312. DOI: 10.1002/asi.23904.

Gwizdka, J. and Mostafa, J. (2017). NeuroIIR: Challenges in bringing neuroscience to re-search in human-information interaction. In *Proceedings of the 2017 Conference on Conference Human Information Interaction and Retrieval* (pp. 437–438). ACM. DOI: 10.1145/3020165.3022165. 48, 52

Gwizdka, J. and Zhang, Y. (2015). Differences in eye-tracking measures between visits and revisits to relevant and irrelevant web pages. In *Proceedings of the 38th International ACM SIGIR Conference on Research and Development in Information Retrieval* (pp. 811–814). ACM. DOI: 10.1145/2766462.2767795. 34, 48

Harvey, M. and Pointon, M. (2017). Searching on the go: the effects of fragmented attention on mobile web search tasks. In *Proceedings of the 40th International ACM SIGIR Confer-ence on Research and Development in Information Retrieval* (pp. 155–164). ACM. DOI: 10.1145/3077136.3080770. 32

He, J. and Yilmaz, E. (2017). User behaviour and task characteristics: A field study of daily infor-mation behaviour. In *Proceedings of the 2017 Conference on Conference Human Information Interaction and Retrieval* (pp. 67–76). ACM. DOI: 10.1145/3020165.3020188. 7, 19, 21, 30, 33

Hong, S. R., Suh, M. M., Henry Riche, N., Lee, J., Kim, J., and Zachry, M. (2018). Collaborative dynamic queries: Supporting distributed small group decision-making. In *Proceedings of the 2018 CHI Conference on Human Factors in Computing Systems* (p. 66). ACM. DOI: 10.1145/3173574.3173640. 12

Htun, N. N., Halvey, M., and Baillie, L. (2017). An interface for supporting asynchronous multi-level collaborative information retrieval. In *Proceedings of the 2017 Conference on*

Conference Human Information Interaction and Retrieval (pp. 225–234). ACM. DOI: 10.1145/3020165.3020172. 46

Huvila, I. (2008). Work and work roles: A context of tasks. *Journal of Documentation*, 64(6), 797–815. DOI: 10.1108/00220410810912406. 39

Ingwersen, P. (1996). Cognitive perspectives of information retrieval interaction: Elements of a cognitive IR theory. *Journal of Documentation*, 52(1), 3–50. DOI: 10.1108/eb026960. 2, 57

Jansen, M., Bos, W., van der Vet, P., Huibers, T., and Hiemstra, D. (2010). TeddIR: Tangible information retrieval for children. In *Proceedings of the 9th International Conference on Interaction Design and Children* (pp. 282–285). ACM. DOI: 10.1145/1810543.1810592. 1

Jiang, J., He, D., and Allan, J. (2014). Searching, browsing, and clicking in a search session: Changes in user behavior by task and over time. In *Proceedings of the 37th International ACM SIGIR Conference on Research and Development in Information Retrieval* (pp. 607–616). ACM. DOI: 10.1145/2600428.2609633. 11

Jiang, J., He, D., and Allan, J. (2017). Comparing in situ and multidimensional relevance judgments. In *Proceedings of the 40th International ACM SIGIR Conference on Research and Development in Information Retrieval* (pp. 405–414). ACM. DOI: 10.1145/3077136.3080840. 3, 13, 48, 49, 53, 61

Jiang, Z., Wen, J. R., Dou, Z., Zhao, W. X., Nie, J. Y., and Yue, M. (2017). Learning to diversify search results via subtopic attention. In *Proceedings of the 40th International ACM SIGIR Conference on Research and Development in Information Retrieval* (pp. 545–554). ACM. DOI: 10.1145/3077136.3080805.

Kamvar, M. and Baluja, S. (2006). A large-scale study of wireless search behavior: Google mobile search. In *Proceedings of the SIGCHI Conference on Human Factors in Computing Systems* (pp. 701–709). ACM. DOI: 10.1145/1124772.1124877. 1

Kato, M. P., Yamamoto, T., Ohshima, H., and Tanaka, K. (2014). Investigating users' query formulations for cognitive search intents. In *Proceedings of the 37th International ACM SIGIR Conference on Research and Development in Information Retrieval* (pp. 577–586). ACM. DOI: 10.1145/2600428.2609566. 7

Kelly, D. (2009). Methods for evaluating interactive information retrieval systems with users. *Foundations and Trends in Information Retrieval*, 3(1–2), 1-224. DOI: 10.1561/1500000012. 1, 2, 7, 8, 9, 10, 12, 20, 21, 27, 38, 57

Kelly, D., Arguello, J., Edwards, A., and Wu, W. C. (2015). Development and evaluation of search tasks for IIR experiments using a cognitive complexity framework. In *Proceedings of the*

2015 International Conference on the Theory of Information Retrieval (pp. 101–110). ACM. DOI: 10.1145/2808194.2809465. 30

Kelly, D. and Azzopardi, L. (2015). How many results per page? A study of serp size, search behavior and user experience. In *Proceedings of the 38th International ACM SIGIR Conference on Research and Development in Information Retrieval* (pp. 183–192). ACM. DOI: 10.1145/2766462.2767732. 21, 43, 46

Kelly, D. and Fu, X. (2006). Elicitation of term relevance feedback: An investigation of term source and context. In *Proceedings of the 29th Annual International ACM SIGIR Conference on Research and Development in Information Retrieval* (pp. 453–460). ACM. DOI: 10.1145/1148170.1148249. 12

Kelly, D. and Sugimoto, C. R. (2013). A systematic review of interactive information retrieval evaluation studies, 1967–2006. *Journal of the American Society for Information Science and Technology*, 64(4), 745–770. DOI: 10.1002/asi.22799. 8, 9, 18, 42, 53, 54

Kim, J., McNally, B., Norooz, L., and Druin, A. (2017). Internet search roles of adults in their homes. In *Proceedings of the 2017 CHI Conference on Human Factors in Computing Systems* (pp. 4948–4959). ACM. DOI: 10.1145/3025453.3025572. 19

Kittur, A., Chi, E. H., and Suh, B. (2008). Crowdsourcing user studies with Mechanical Turk. In *Proceedings of the SIGCHI Conference on Human Factors in Computing Systems* (pp. 453–456). ACM. DOI: 10.1145/1357054.1357127. 29

Klouche, K., Ruotsalo, T., Cabral, D., Andolina, S., Bellucci, A., and Jacucci, G. (2015). Designing for exploratory search on touch devices. In *Proceedings of the 33rd Annual ACM Conference on Human Factors in Computing Systems* (pp. 4189–4198). ACM. DOI: 10.1145/2702123.2702489. 43

Lagun, D. and Agichtein, E. (2015). Inferring searcher attention by jointly modeling user interactions and content salience. In *Proceedings of the 38th International ACM SIGIR Conference on Research and Development in Information Retrieval* (pp. 483–492). ACM. DOI: 10.1145/2766462.2767745. 18

Lagun, D., Hsieh, C. H., Webster, D., and Navalpakkam, V. (2014). Towards better measurement of attention and satisfaction in mobile search. In *Proceedings of the 37th International ACM SIGIR Conference on Research and Development in Information Retrieval* (pp. 113–122). ACM. DOI: 10.1145/2600428.2609631. 8, 47

Law, E., Yin, M., Goh, J., Chen, K., Terry, M. A., and Gajos, K. Z. (2016). Curiosity killed the cat, but makes crowdwork better. In *Proceedings of the 2016 CHI Conference on Human Factors in Computing Systems* (pp. 4098–4110). ACM. DOI: 10.1145/2858036.2858144. 29

Li, Y. (2009). Exploring the relationships between work task and search task in information search. *Journal of the American Society for information Science and Technology*, 60(2), 275–291. DOI: 10.1002/asi.20977. 30

Li, Y. and Belkin, N. J. (2010). An exploration of the relationships between work task and interactive information search behavior. *Journal of the American Society for Information Science and Technology*, 61(9), 1771-1789. DOI: 10.1002/asi.21359. 30

Li, Y. and Belkin, N. J. (2008). A faceted approach to conceptualizing tasks in information seeking. *Information Processing and Management*, 44(6), 1822–1837. DOI: 10.1016/j.ipm.2008.07.005. 15, 23, 30

Li, Y., Dong, A., Wang, H., Deng, H., Chang, Y., and Zhai, C. (2014). A two-dimensional click model for query auto-completion. In *Proceedings of the 37th International ACM SIGIR Conference on Research and Development in Information Retrieval* (pp. 455–464). ACM. DOI: 10.1145/2600428.2609571. 52

Liu, C., Belkin, N. J., and Cole, M. J. (2012). Personalization of search results using interaction behaviors in search sessions. In *Proceedings of the 35th International ACM SIGIR Conference on Research and Development in Information Retrieval* (pp. 205–214). ACM. DOI: 10.1145/2348283.2348314. 7

Liu, J. (2017). Toward a unified model of human information behavior: an equilibrium perspective. *Journal of Documentation*, 73(4), 666–688. DOI: 10.1108/JD-06-2016-0080. 39, 52, 53

Liu, J. (2019). A reference-dependent model of search evaluation. In *Proceedings of the 2019 International ACM SIGIR Conference on Human Information Interaction and Retrieval* (pp. 405–408). ACM. DOI: 10.1145/3295750.3298970. 52, 53

Liu, J., Cole, M. J., Liu, C., Bierig, R., Gwizdka, J., Belkin, N. J., Zhang, J. and Zhang, X. (2010). Search behaviors in different task types. In *Proceedings of the 10th Annual Joint Conference on Digital Libraries* (pp. 69–78). ACM. DOI: 10.1145/1816123.1816134. 21, 27, 30

Liu, M., Liu, Y., Mao, J., Luo, C., Zhang, M., and Ma, S. (2018). "Satisfaction with failure" or" unsatisfied success": Investigating the relationship between search success and user satisfaction. In *Proceedings of the 2018 World Wide Web Conference (WWW'18)* (pp. 1533–1542). DOI: 10.1145/3178876.3186065. 26

Liu, J., Mitsui, M., Belkin, N. J., and Shah, C. (2019). Task, information seeking intentions, and user behavior: Toward a multi-level understanding of Web search. In *Proceedings of the 2019 Conference on Human Information Interaction and Retrieval* (pp. 123–132). ACM. DOI: 10.1145/3295750.3298922. 7, 21, 42

Liu, Y. H. and Wacholder, N. (2017). Evaluating the impact of MeSH (Medical Subject Headings) terms on different types of searchers. *Information Processing and Management*, 53(4), 851–870. DOI: 10.1016/j.ipm.2017.03.004. 20

Luo, C., Liu, Y., Sakai, T., Zhang, F., Zhang, M., and Ma, S. (2017). Evaluating mobile search with height-biased gain. In *Proceedings of the 40th International ACM SIGIR Conference on Research and Development in Information Retrieval* (pp. 435–444). ACM. DOI: 10.1145/3077136.3080795. 48, 49

Luo, J., Zhang, S., and Yang, H. (2014). Win-win search: Dual-agent stochastic game in session search. In *Proceedings of the 37th International ACM SIGIR Conference on Research and Development in Information Retrieval* (pp. 587–596). ACM. DOI: 10.1145/2600428.2609629. 3

Mao, J., Liu, Y., Kando, N., Zhang, M., and Ma, S. (2018). How does domain expertise affect users' search interaction and outcome in exploratory search? *ACM Transactions on Information Systems (TOIS)*, 36(4), 42. DOI: 10.1145/3223045. 20

Mao, J., Liu, Y., Zhou, K., Nie, J. Y., Song, J., Zhang, M., Ma, S., Sun, J. and Luo, H. (2016). When does relevance mean usefulness and user satisfaction in web search? In *Proceedings of the 39th International ACM SIGIR Conference on Research and Development in Information Retrieval* (pp. 463–472). ACM. DOI: 10.1145/2911451.2911507. 13, 49

Mitsui, M., Liu, J., Belkin, N. J., and Shah, C. (2017). Predicting information seeking intentions from search behaviors. In *Proceedings of the 40th International ACM SIGIR Conference on Research and Development in Information Retrieval* (pp. 1121–1124). ACM. DOI: 10.1145/3077136.3080737. 30

Moffat, A., Bailey, P., Scholer, F., and Thomas, P. (2017). Incorporating user expectations and behavior into the measurement of search effectiveness. *ACM Transactions on Information Systems (TOIS)*, 35(3), 24. DOI: 10.1145/3052768. 12

Morris, M. R., Fourney, A., Ali, A., and Vonessen, L. (2018). Understanding the needs of searchers with dyslexia. In *Proceedings of the 2018 CHI Conference on Human Factors in Computing Systems* (p. 35). ACM. DOI: 10.1145/3173574.3173609. 19

Moshfeghi, Y. and Jose, J. M. (2013). An effective implicit relevance feedback technique using affective, physiological and behavioural features. In *Proceedings of the 36th International ACM SIGIR Conference on Research and Development in Information Retrieval* (pp. 133–142). ACM. DOI: 10.1145/2484028.2484074. 48

Moshfeghi, Y., Triantafillou, P., and Pollick, F. E. (2016). Understanding information need: An fMRI study. In *Proceedings of the 39th International ACM SIGIR Conference on Research and Development in Information Retrieval* (pp. 335–344). ACM. DOI: 10.1145/2911451.2911534. 2, 8, 28, 34, 59

Nicholson, J., Huber, M., Jackson, D., and Olivier, P. (2014). Panopticon as an eLearning support search tool. In *Proceedings of the SIGCHI Conference on Human Factors in Computing Systems* (pp. 1221–1224). ACM. DOI: 10.1145/2556288.2557082. 31

O'Brien, H. L. and McCay-Peet, L. (2017). Asking good questions: Questionnaire design and analysis in interactive information retrieval research. In *Proceedings of the 2017 Conference on Conference Human Information Interaction and Retrieval* (pp. 27–36). ACM. DOI: 10.1145/3020165.3020167. 3

Ong, K., Järvelin, K., Sanderson, M., and Scholer, F. (2017). Using information scent to understand mobile and desktop web search behavior. In *Proceedings of the 40th International ACM SIGIR Conference on Research and Development in Information Retrieval* (pp. 295–304). ACM. DOI: 10.1145/3077136.3080817. 7, 11, 19, 26, 32, 43

Robertson, S. (2008). On the history of evaluation in IR. *Journal of Information Science*, 34(4), 439–456. DOI: 10.1177/0165551507086989. xvi, 3, 5, 58

Ruotsalo, T., Peltonen, J., Eugster, M. J., Głowacka, D., Floréen, P., Myllymäki, P., Jacucci, G., and Kaski, S. (2018). Interactive intent modeling for exploratory search. *ACM Transactions on Information Systems (TOIS)*, 36(4), 44. DOI: 10.1145/3231593. 26, 31, 43

Ruthven, I. (2008). Interactive information retrieval. *Annual Review of Information Science and Technology*, 42(1), 43–91. DOI: 10.1002/aris.2008.1440420109. 7, 13

Sakai, T. (2016). Statistical significance, power, and sample sizes: A systematic review of SIGIR and *TOIS*, 2006-2015. In *Proceedings of the 39th International ACM SIGIR Conference on Research and Development in Information Retrieval* (pp. 5–14). ACM. DOI: 10.1145/2911451.2911492. 9, 29, 37, 42, 53, 54, 57

Sanderson, M. and Zobel, J. (2005). Information retrieval system evaluation: Effort, sensitivity, and reliability. In *Proceedings of the 28th Annual International ACM SIGIR Conference on Research and Development in Information Retrieval* (pp. 162–169). ACM. DOI: 10.1145/1076034.1076064. 9

Saracevic, T. (1975). Relevance: A review of and a framework for the thinking on the notion in information science. *Journal of the American Society for Information Science*, 26(6), 321–343. DOI: 10.1002/asi.4630260604. 47

Shah, C. (2018). Information fostering-Being proactive with information seeking and retrieval: Perspective paper. In *Proceedings of the 2018 Conference on Human Information Interaction and Retrieval* (pp. 62–71). ACM. DOI: 10.1145/3176349.3176389. 7

Shah, C. and Marchionini, G. (2010). Awareness in collaborative information seeking. *Journal of the American Society for Information Science and Technology*, 61(10), 1970–1986. DOI: 10.1002/asi.21379. 12

Shah, C., Pickens, J., and Golovchinsky, G. (2010). Role-based results redistribution for collaborative information retrieval. *Information Processing and Management*, 46(6), 773–781. DOI: 10.1016/j.ipm.2009.10.002. 43

Singla, A., White, R., and Huang, J. (2010). Studying trailfinding algorithms for enhanced web search. In *Proceedings of the 33rd International ACM SIGIR Conference on Research and Development in Information Retrieval* (pp. 443–450). ACM. DOI: 10.1145/1835449.1835524. 18

Smith, C. L., Gwizdka, J., and Feild, H. (2017). The use of query auto-completion over the course of search sessions with multifaceted information needs. *Information Processing and Management*, 53(5), 1139–1155. DOI: 10.1016/j.ipm.2017.05.001. 20

Smucker, M. D. and Jethani, C. P. (2010). Human performance and retrieval precision revisited. In *Proceedings of the 33rd International ACM SIGIR Conference on Research and Development in Information Retrieval* (pp. 595–602). ACM. DOI: 10.1145/1835449.1835549. 48

Song, Y., Ma, H., Wang, H., and Wang, K. (2013). Exploring and exploiting user search behavior on mobile and tablet devices to improve search relevance. In *Proceedings of the 22nd International Conference on World Wide Web* (pp. 1201–1212). ACM. DOI: 10.1145/2488388.2488493. 32

Spink, A., Yang, Y., Jansen, J., Nykanen, P., Lorence, D. P., Ozmutlu, S., and Ozmutlu, H. C. (2004). A study of medical and health queries to web search engines. *Health Information and Libraries Journal*, 21(1), 44–51. DOI: 10.1111/j.1471-1842.2004.00481.x. 3

Sun, S. and Belkin, N. J. (2015). Information attribute motivators of personal health information management activities. In *Proceedings of the 78th ASIS&T Annual Meeting* (pp. 1–9). DOI: 10.1002/pra2.2015.145052010046. 21

Suominen, H., Kelly, L., Goeuriot, L., Névéol, A., Ramadier, L., Robert, A., Kanoulas, E., Spijker, R., Azzopardi, L., Li, D., Palotti, J., and Zuccon, G. (2018). Overview of the CLEF eHealth evaluation lab 2018. In *International Conference of the Cross-Language Evaluation Forum for European Languages* (pp. 286–301). Springer, Cham. DOI: 10.1007/978-3-319-98932-7_26. 55

Syed, R. and Collins-Thompson, K. (2017). Retrieval algorithms optimized for human learning. In *Proceedings of the 40th International ACM SIGIR Conference on Research and Development in Information Retrieval* (pp. 555–564). ACM. DOI: 10.1145/3077136.3080835. 12, 31, 46, 47

Teevan, J., Dumais, S. T., and Horvitz, E. (2007). Characterizing the value of personalizing search. In *Proceedings of the 30th Annual International ACM SIGIR Conference on Research and Development in Information Retrieval* (pp. 757–758). ACM. DOI: 10.1145/1277741.1277894. 15

Teevan, J., Dumais, S. T., and Horvitz, E. (2010). Potential for personalization. *ACM Transactions on Computer-Human Interaction*, 17(1), 4. DOI: 10.1145/1721831.1721835. 15

Trippas, J. R., Spina, D., Cavedon, L., Joho, H., and Sanderson, M. (2018). Informing the design of spoken conversational search: Perspective paper. In *Proceedings of the 2018 International ACM SIGIR Conference on Human Information Interaction and Retrieval* (pp. 32–41). ACM. DOI: 10.1145/3176349.3176387. 1

Turpin, L., Kelly, D., and Arguello, J. (2016). To blend or not to blend? Perceptual speed, visual memory and aggregated search. In *Proceedings of the 39th International ACM SIGIR Conference on Research and Development in Information Retrieval* (pp. 1021–1024). ACM. DOI: 10.1145/2911451.2914739. 43

Umemoto, K., Yamamoto, T., and Tanaka, K. (2016). Scentbar: A query suggestion interface visualizing the amount of missed relevant information for intrinsically diverse search. In *Proceedings of the 39th International ACM SIGIR conference on Research and Development in Information Retrieval* (pp. 405–414). ACM. DOI: 10.1145/2911451.2911546. 43, 46, 47

Vtyurina, A. and Fourney, A. (2018). Exploring the role of conversational cues in guided task support with virtual assistants. In *Proceedings of the 2018 CHI Conference on Human Factors in Computing Systems* (p. 208). ACM. DOI: 10.1145/3173574.3173782. 19

Wan, X., Li, H., and Xiao, J. (2010). EUSUM: extracting easy-to-understand English summaries for non-native readers. In *Proceedings of the 33rd International ACM SIGIR Conference on Research and Development in Information Retrieval* (pp. 491–498). ACM. DOI: 10.1145/1835449.1835532. 18, 21

Wang, Y., Sarkar, S., and Shah, C. (2018). Juggling with information sources, task type, and information quality. In *Proceedings of the 2018 Conference on Human Information Interaction and Retrieval* (pp. 82–91). ACM. DOI: 10.1145/3176349.3176390. 19

White, R. W. (2018). Skill discovery in virtual assistants. *Communications of the ACM*, 61(11), 106–113. DOI: 10.1145/3185336. 1

Wilson, M. L., Chi, E. H., Reeves, S., and Coyle, D. (2014). RepliCHI: the workshop II. In *CHI'14 Extended Abstracts on Human Factors in Computing Systems* (pp. 33–36). ACM. DOI: 10.1145/2559206.2559233. 55

Xie, I., Joo, S., and Bennett-Kapusniak, R. (2017). User involvement and system support in applying search tactics. *Journal of the Association for Information Science and Technology*, 68(5), 1165–1185. DOI: 10.1002/asi.23765. 19

Xu, H., Wang, J., Hua, X. S., and Li, S. (2010). Image search by concept map. In *Proceedings of the 33rd International ACM SIGIR Conference on Research and Development in Information Retrieval* (pp. 275–282). ACM. DOI: 10.1145/1835449.1835497. 12

Yamamoto, Y. and Yamamoto, T. (2018). Query priming for promoting critical thinking in web search. In *Proceedings of the 2018 Conference on Human Information Interaction and Retrieval* (pp. 12–21). ACM. DOI: 10.1145/3176349.3176377. 21, 31

Yuan, X. and Belkin, N. J. (2007). Supporting multiple information-seeking strategies in a single system framework. In *Proceedings of the 30th Annual International ACM SIGIR Conference on Research and Development in Information Retrieval* (pp. 247–254). ACM. DOI: 10.1145/1277741.1277786. 12

Zhang, X., Liu, J., Cole, M., and Belkin, N. (2015). Predicting users' domain knowledge in information retrieval using multiple regression analysis of search behaviors. *Journal of the Association for Information Science and Technology*, 66(5), 980–1000. DOI: 10.1002/asi.23218. 27, 30

Zhang, Y., Zhang, J., Lease, M., and Gwizdka, J. (2014). Multidimensional relevance modeling via psychometrics and crowdsourcing. In *Proceedings of the 37th International ACM SIGIR Conference on Research and Development in Information Retrieval* (pp. 435–444). ACM. DOI: 10.1145/2600428.2609577. 11, 29, 47

Zhao, Y. and Zhu, Q. (2014). Evaluation on crowdsourcing research: Current status and future direction. *Information Systems Frontiers*, 16(3), 417–434. DOI: 10.1007/s10796-012-9350-4. 29

Authors' Biographies

Jiqun Liu is a Ph.D. candidate in the Department of Library and Information Science at School of Communication and Information, Rutgers University. His main research interests lie in understanding how people's problematic situations, information seeking intentions, and search strategies are connected in search interactions and what this means for the design and evaluation of user-centered interactive search systems. Jiqun Liu received his M.S. in Information Science from the Department of Information Management, Peking University and a double B.S. in Library Science and Finance from the Business School, Nankai University.

Chirag Shah is an Associate Professor in both the School of Communication and Information (SC&I) and the Department of Computer Science at Rutgers University. His research interests include studies of interactive information retrieval/seeking, trying to understand the task a person is doing, and providing proactive recommendations. Dr. Shah received his M.S. in Computer Science from University of Massachusetts (UMass) at Amherst, and Ph.D. in Information Science from University of North Carolina (UNC) at Chapel Hill. He directs the InfoSeeking Lab at Rutgers University where he investigates issues related to information seeking, human-computer interaction (HCI), and social media, supported by grants from National Science Foundation (NSF), National Institute of Health (NIH), Institute of Museum and Library Services (IMLS), Amazon, Google, and Yahoo. More information about Dr. Shah can be found at http://chiragshah.org/.